Keeping the Struggle Alive

Studying Desegregation in Our Town

A Guide to Doing Oral History

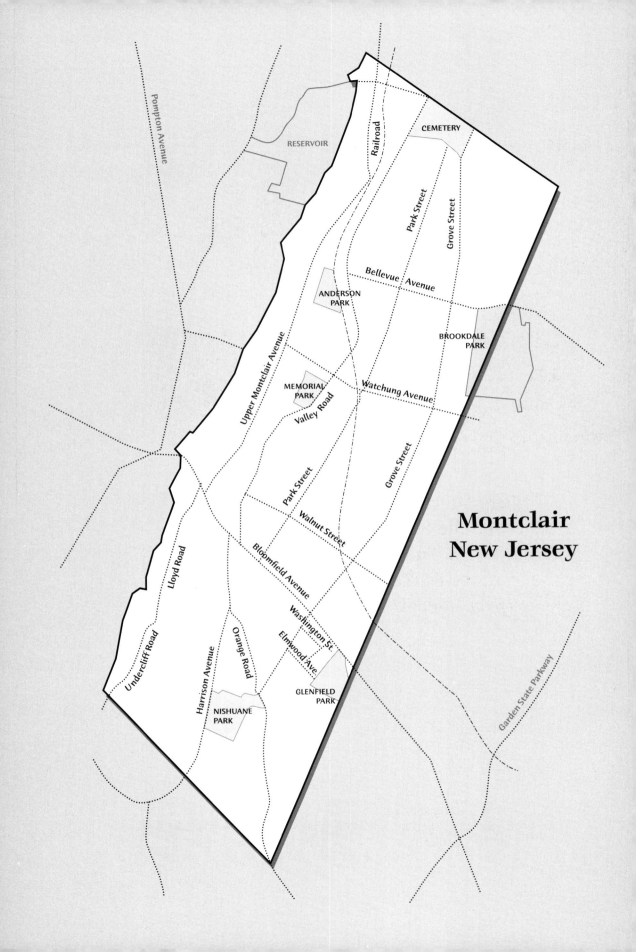

Montclair
New Jersey

Pompton Avenue

RESERVOIR

Railroad

CEMETERY

Park Street

Grove Street

Bellevue   Avenue

ANDERSON PARK

BROOKDALE PARK

Upper Montclair Avenue

MEMORIAL PARK

Watchung Avenue

Valley Road

Grove Street

Park Street

Walnut Street

Bloomfield Avenue

Lloyd Road

Washington St

Undercliff Road

Harrison Avenue

Orange Road

Elmwood Ave

GLENFIELD PARK

NISHUANE PARK

Garden State Parkway

Keeping the Struggle Alive

Studying Desegregation in Our Town

A Guide to Doing Oral History

Bernadette Anand
Michelle Fine
David S. Surrey
Tiffany Perkins
and the Renaissance School Class of 2000

Foreword by Arthur Kinoy

Teachers College Press
Teachers College, Columbia University
New York and London

NMSA

National Middle School
Association

Published by Teachers College Press, 1234 Amsterdam Avenue,
New York, NY 10027

This research and publication were generously supported by the Spencer Foundation and the Carnegie Foundation.

Historical photographs on pages 13, 16, 18–19, 70, and 76 are reproduced from the
collections of the Library of Congress.

Library of Congress Cataloging-in-Publication Data

Keeping the struggle alive : studying desegregation in our town : a guide to doing
oral history / Bernadette Anand…[et al.].
    p. cm.
  Includes bibliographical references and index.
  ISBN 0-8077-4145-0 (pbk.)
  1. School integraton—New Jersey—Montclair—History—20th century. 2. Oral
history. 3. Renaissance Middle School (Montclair, N.J.) I. Anand, Bernadette.
LC214.23.M65 K44 2002
379.2′63′0974931—dc21   2001052283

ISBN 0-8077-4145-0

Printed on acid-free paper
Manufactured in the United States of America

09 08 07 06 05 04 03 02   8 7 6 5 4 3 2 1

Contents

To contact us...
PHONE: David Goodwin,
City Editor
(973) 877-4136
FAX: (973) 877-5845
E-MAIL: dgoodwin@starledger.com
WEB: http://www.nj.com/essex

Essex
Sunday Star-Ledger

OW

Once upon a time in Montclair schools

Oral history project teaches pupils story of desegregation

By Jeffery C. Mays
STAR-LEDGER STAFF

When Jane Manners was a student in Montclair, she thought nothing of having African-American and Latino classmates. It was a different story with some of her classmates at Harvard.

"I talked to my college roommates, many of whom grew up in these lily-white, old-money towns, and found they had such segregated experiences," said Manners, who is white. "I was one of the few who had gone to an integrated school."

That's why Manners, who wrote her senior thesis on the history of the integration of Montclair schools, didn't hesitate to return to her old stomping grounds to talk to pupils in Renaissance Middle School, after she learned they were working on an oral history about desegregation efforts in the Essex County town.

"What was it like under segregation?" asked a black pupil.

"Was it okay to have friends in different schools and play sports with them?" a white pupil asked.

Manners, 23, sitting in the center of the classroom Friday surrounded by a diverse mix of seventh-graders, answered each question fully and thoroughly. She never spoke down to

PLEASE SEE **MONTCLAIR, PAGE 52**

PHOTO BY JERRY McCREA

Evan Richardson, left, questions Jane Manners, back to camera, about Montclair school desegregation during a class Friday. Manners, who grew up in Montclair and wrote her senior thesis at Harvard University on the topic, was helping seventh-graders at Renaissance School with an oral history project.

Foreword

As with all struggle, the struggle for civil rights was the struggle of specific individuals in their specific communities. The local struggles and cases that involved me around the country in civil rights conflicts were the experiences that motivated students in my classes at Rutgers University School of Law in Newark to commit themselves to the ongoing battles for the enforcement of constitutional civil rights.

In 1973 when we bought our home in Montclair, its struggle for school integration was a hot local issue and influenced our decision to live here. The landmark ruling of *Brown* v. *Board of Education* mandating school integration had, at first, made the school bus a symbol of force, not choice. In Montclair, however, the struggle for school integration was resolved through an innovative "magnet school" program where students willingly boarded buses to attend schools of their own choosing. This magnet program would later be replicated in many communities to meet federal requirements.

The ruling on school integration put students in the forefront of the Civil Rights Movement. In the candid stories of the 1960s recorded by students of Renaissance Middle School in this book, you will find how Montclair's young people, too, were deeply involved in the struggle.

During the past few years, I have had the opportunity to get directly involved in Montclair's local issues and in community life. One of the activities that provided me great pleasure was sharing my experiences with Montclair's school children. Renaissance Middle School, just a block away from our home, asked me to help frame this project in its national context. The project has made history alive for our young people as well as for those who were interviewed. I also have several young neighborhood friends who run up to me occasionally with an enthusiastic, "Arthur, Mr. Arthur!"

My hope is that this oral history project, like Montclair's magnet school plan, will be replicated in other communities to help keep the memory of the Civil Rights Movement alive. This book is a major effort in that direction. It is a valuable instrument in the teaching of recent critically important history to the younger generation, and will be extremely useful to educators, parents, and community activists throughout the country who will be accepting this deep responsibility.

Arthur Kinoy
Montclair, NJ

Introduction

> It is necessary and even urgent
> that the school become a space to gather and engender certain
> democratic dispositions, such as the disposition to listen to
> others—not as a favor but as a duty—and to respect them.
> Paulo Freire, *Teachers as Cultural Workers*

STUDENTS IN A MONTCLAIR, NEW JERSEY, public middle school learned about their community's history of desegregation through a year-long language arts and social studies project involving a rigorous examination of nonprint materials, newspaper articles, and historical documents, as well as developing, conducting, and analyzing interviews of the town residents who participated in this struggle. This book represents the story of how 75 seventh graders at the Renaissance Middle School and four educators (Bernadette, Michelle, Tiffany, and David) searched for a community's chronicles of inequity as well as possibilities for change. It honors each of the voices the students discovered for their civic courage and the integrated magnet school system they helped create. It is a history of how one northern community, albeit reluctantly, joined the national Civil Rights Movement and eventually added its personal and moral responses to injustice. Most important, it is a journey of a group of students and adults who engaged in a highly critical reading of the word through their re-reading of "their" worlds (Freire, 1998).

It is important to talk about teacher-created projects and critical student inquiry work for two reasons. First, educators face a number of different threats to their own empowerment and roles as intellectual leaders and competent developers of curricula and forms of pedagogy (Aronowitz & Giroux, 1993). Standards and assessments are imposed from without. High-stake tests reward and punish students, teachers, and administrators rather than offer them opportunities for development

(Meier, 1995). School districts purchase packaged programs that control classroom time, content, and practices for the purposes of maintaining the schools as sites of reproduction rather than resistance. With moves toward privatization and vouchers, private interest groups are assuming control over public schools, managing them as businesses. Questions of equity, access, and separation of church and state, foundational to democratic schooling, are treated as if they are trivial. With the testing mania, students find themselves less involved in critical inquiry and the exercise of democracy. Authoritarian practices emerge ever more, ironically in the name of standards or accountability, drowning out the authority of students, teachers, and communities.

Second, the rising recognition of hate crimes, racial profiling, xenophobia, and police harassment in communities of color, and the national retreat from affirmative action once considered a fixture in the landscape of the struggle for equity, are strong indicators of the "dismantling of desegregation" (Orfield, Easton, & the Harvard Project on School Desegregation, 1996) and the erosion of a dream of racial justice. These trends make it imperative for all students to be engaged critically in understanding the history of racism in the United States and the history and potential power of social struggle (Bell, 1987). To take up this work in public schools is to challenge what we teach, how we teach, how we assess, and what we ask students to interrogate.

> Culturally relevant pedagogues take the students' real lives seriously. Students' day-to-day experiences become an essential building block for the curriculum. Rather than rely on district-mandated texts, the teachers ask students to bring their experiences into the classroom and help them learn necessary skills in the contexts of their lives. Mathematics and literacy are tied to real life problems students encounter.
>
> Gloria Ladson-Billings,
> "Who Will Survive America?"

Our oral history project on the desegregation of the town's schools challenged students' sense of justice. It also propelled us as educators to move beyond passive criteria of compliance and measurable achievement. We had to think critically about the significance of the New Jersey Core Standards for Language Arts Literacy and Social Studies. We examined these standards and connected them to issues of segregation, integration, and the history of the Civil Rights Movement on a national, state, and community level. We knew that if students were expected to "acquire geographical understanding by studying human systems in geography and how they are significant (New Jersey Department of Education, 1996, PTM 1400.06)," we could breathe life into the standard by having the students look at the racial and social patterns of housing and schooling that exist in their community and in the nation.

In this work we came to see vividly and challenge historically the cutting power of "tracks," in communities and in schools, literally and symbolically signifying and stabilizing the "haves" and the "have nots," always demarcating and separating (Foster, 1997; Oakes, 1985; Wheelock, 1992). In schools, we witness the entrenched tracks of intellectual partitions, rarely crossed, deeply defining, indeed scarring. Like radical geographers, educators understand that tracks are spatial metaphors that work to split and painfully and deceptively tell people who they are, who they can become, who they aren't, who they will never be. Educators know all too well the intimate ways in which the geography of schools and communities comes to be inscribed on the bodies and minds of youth. Tracks in schools are the Mason-Dixon borders of geography and pedagogy, opportunity and identity. Educators know that, as do youth. This is a book about what it means to invite students, in a racially integrated and explicitly detracked middle school, to interrogate the tracks of history that have severed their town and schools, deepening and sustaining class, ethnic, and racial divisions.

As educators, all the authors have spent our professional lifetimes challenging the very stratifications cemented by tracks. We have committed our work, in middle and high schools, and in college and graduate training, to what might be called "detracking"—that is, the creation of educational communities in which rigor and critical inquiry are joined; the joys of rich educational practice are accessible to all; and class, ethnic, and racial diversity are delightful opportunities, not a reason to separate. We are privileged to live and work in a town in which every morning, yellow buses calmly and routinely escort children over the tracks of residential segregation into integrated schools, and to teach in a school born of the desire to defy tracks and educate all at high levels.

We undertook this project with middle school youth to carve out an opportunity to delve, historically, into a biography of tracks in one northern community, with a hope that this project could speak to educators, youth, and communities all over the nation. These middle school students had the opportunity to join with us in an oral history project, interviewing and unearthing the voices of struggle that fought so hard to desegregate the schools in the North. We learned how everyday people became activists, and that a bus could symbolize political struggle and then victory. We learned, too, that middle school youth—across class and race lines—could become brilliant social historians; that oral history has the potential to make a classroom come alive with the intelligence of diverse students; and that the struggle for full integration is never over.

> I can only say once more that situations have to be deliberately created in order for students to break free in this way. Coming together in their pluralities and their differences, they may finally articulate how they are choosing themselves and what the projects are by means of which they can identify themselves. We all need to recognize each other in our striving, our becoming, our invention of the possible. And yet, it is a question of acting in the light of a vision of what might be a vision that enables people to perceive the voids, take heed of the violations and move (if they can) to repair. Such a vision, we have found, can be enlarged and enriched by those on the margins, whoever they are.
>
> Maxine Greene, "Diversity and Inclusion"

We designed this oral history project to be intimately local and then provocatively global; but foremost so that it would connect our students, historically and today, to their community and the history of activism that constitutes this community. We knew that if young people spent time with the "everyday heroes" of Montclair, they would come to recognize the power in working for social justice and to witness the change one individual can make in establishing a more equitable society. We were committed to the principles of democratic schooling—theory and practice based on experience (Dewey, 1938)—and kept this tenet at the core of the course design. The interviews scheduled throughout the year presented the students with the opportunity to design their own questions, reflect on the responses, and then analyze the ideas and perspectives they heard with what they already knew from their reading.

Language arts and social studies teachers who engage in team teaching and interdisciplinary work will find the course outlined in these pages helpful in the planning and design of projects that integrate strong social processes into reading and writing. The book, through the process described and the content produced, is written as well for teachers in the fields of community studies, contemporary history, oral history, civil rights, teacher education, and curriculum development.

The first section describes the oral history project and the teaching opportunities that emerged from our conversations about race. Part II, "You Can't Give Up the Struggle" is a history of Northern integration, a retelling of Montclair's school desegregation efforts, interspersed with interviews by the students. Finally, the last section contains a teacher's guide to the project, offering curricular and thematic links.

As educators and learners we have the awesome responsibility of discovering together with our students the stories of the communities we work in and then connecting them to our present situations. This book is an invitation to join with us and other "culturally relevant pedagogues countering the systematic destruction of...cultures that traditional schooling supports" (Ladson-Billings, 1998, p. 299) and bringing the power of all voices into the classroom through specific moments in history. With this small book, we seek to be in conversation, at once, with youth across the country, in integrated and segregated communities, engaged in their own local discoveries; with those youth and educators who struggle for integration in a nation that is fleeing its responsibilities for racial justice; with those who yearn for high academic standards of rigor for all; and with educators who work through an ethic of social justice, pedagogical courage, and engagement with community because they assume, simply, that that is the work they were meant to perform. And so we write with a sense of commitment and awe for educators and youth who dare to imagine what is not yet—and what must be (Greene, 1995).

Bernadette Anand
Michelle Fine
David S. Surrey
Tiffany Perkins

Former Governor Jim Florio of New Jersey and Dr. Mary Lee Fitzgerald in the auditorium of Hillside School, Montclair. Dr. Fitzgerald, former superintendent of the Montclair Public Schools, has just been introduced as the New Jersey Commissioner of Education.

Re-Examining History with Middle School Students

EACH MORNING, 10 YELLOW SCHOOL BUSES end their circuit through Montclair, New Jersey to drop off 149 of Renaissance Middle School's 225 students. Ali, grandson of Charles and Marjorie Baskerville, is among the group of students who arrive by bus. Ali's grandparents and other community activists fought long and hard for school integration and Ali's right to attend a school of his own choosing, and throughout the public school system the buses make this choice possible. To those who retain the memory of struggle, Montclair's school buses and their routes, almost 30 years old, are a regular reminder of the magnet school plan implemented in 1973.

We wondered if any of our 225 students recognized the buses as visible symbols of victory and accomplishment for their own families, friends, and neighbors who, like Ali's grandparents, brought integration to the Montclair public school system. We wondered what it would take in the classroom to show the students that the South wasn't the only place where this struggle occurred, that Montclair went through its own history of desegregation...

The project we describe in this book emerged out of thinking about Fridays. While the Monday through Thursday schedule at Renaissance Middle School covers the traditional distribution of curriculum, Fridays are dedicated to 9-week cycles of 2-hour sessions of in-depth work on aviation, genetics, building bridges, community service, and this, the oral history project. Because the school is thematically organized around core notions of justice, history, social movements, and "renaissances"

A version of this essay was printed in *Radical Teacher*, 2000, Volume 57.

(that is, Italian, Harlem, and Montclair), it seemed fitting to structure an oral history project around the deep, contested history of desegregation of the Montclair public schools.

Renaissance School, like all schools in Montclair, enjoys rich racial and ethnic diversity as a court-ordered site for desegregation. As of this writing, the school is just 3 years old, with 225 sixth, seventh, and eighth graders, balanced evenly by gender and by race, with African American and White the primary "racial" codes relied on by the district. Social-class diversity also characterizes the student body, with just under 20% of students eligible for free or reduced lunch. When the district recognized the need for a new, small middle school, the Superintendent approached Dr. Bernadette Anand, who at that point was respected in the district as a teacher and a principal, a radical critic of tracking, and a progressive educator for equity, student-based inquiry, and multiculturalism.

Renaissance is organized as a project-based, interdisciplinary school. Explicitly detracked, the school, with a day that extends from 8 a.m. to 4 p.m., is relentlessly dedicated to providing strong academic supports so that all students can engage in meaningful inquiry-based work. In this school, budget and personnel are directed primarily at instruction. The school is low on frills and high on adult bodies—teachers, community adults, adjuncts, and volunteering parents. In a state recognized as the fourth most racially segregated in the nation, in a town well known for its racially integrated schools, and in a school committed at once to serious intellectual work, student-based inquiry, and racial/class equity, the civil rights oral history project seemed a natural.

As progressive educators, eager for students to engage with historic and contemporary struggles for race and class justice, with Bernadette Anand as principal and Michelle Fine as parent/volunteer, we worked together to construct the course in that uneasy balance between educator-structured and student-directed. In order to immerse the four cycles of students quickly in the history of the struggle, we arranged to have the *Montclair Times* scanned, from 1947 to 1972, for articles relevant to desegregation. With this mini-archive in hand, at the beginning of each 9-week cycle, students reviewed one or two articles individually and then produced a time line as a class. From the creation of the time line forward, the structure of the course evolved based on student interest. Students read the articles and then identified people they wanted to interview. They designed the interview questions. They coded and analyzed the interview materials. Finally, they decided to publish a book. In this section, we chronicle the course and identify key critical turning points and unresolved issues.

The oral history project comes out of a school in which social justice and student inquiry are central. Students have interrogated the Italian Renaissance and the Harlem Renaissance, and are now moving into the Montclair Renaissance. All of their courses reflect critical perspectives on curriculum and pedagogy. This course is not, politically or pedagogically, a departure from the ethical or intellectual stance of the school. As they move forward, students know, hopefully, a bit more about local history and about themselves as excavators of a history rarely told. Reflecting critically on where their town has been, they can project creatively on where it needs to go.

On the first day of each cycle, students reviewed the local newspaper articles tracing Montclair's history of segregation and integration, lawsuits, "riots," the School Board plans for incremental integration, the denials of racism, the development of magnet schools and tracking, as well as the stubbornly persistent racial and economic class gaps in academic achievement. As they reviewed the newspapers, students began to ask questions along these lines.

- "Why is the Black Student Association protest called a riot—but when the White parents get together to fight integration it's just a parents' meeting?"
- "This town is racially segregated but also by wealth. Which was the problem?"
- "Why do we still sit separately in the lunchroom?"
- "Did the kids have a problem with integration or was it just the parents?"

After some initial instruction and discussion, students were quick to point out the biases of the articles, the journalistic "slants" that accompanied the reporting of the "facts." Some students, particularly a few African American boys, noticed a disparaging tone toward African American "student protests" in the paper, which was lacking in the paper's descriptions of White parents' "meetings." Others noted the frequent placement of articles about the Black Student Association near articles about a liquor store or a drug bust. A few commented that "winners usually write the history." Others concluded, "That's why we have to do this project." Even in the early stages of the project, conflicts arose as we discussed past controversies. Thus we set a distinct tone—one of respect for all points of view.

Before the interviews began, we watched portions of *Eyes on the Prize* (1986), read *Freedom's Children* (Levine, 1993), and discussed these histories of racism in Arkansas and Alabama. Students were shocked by the brutality of Little Rock and awed by the strength exhibited by protestors and those who refused to take "no" for an answer. (To see a celebration of the 40th anniverary of the integration of Little Rock High School, see *http://www.centralhigh57.org*.) The class then listened to Montclair's own Arthur Kinoy, civil rights activist and lawyer, who riveted us with national and local stories of oppression, resistance, and McCarthyism. Punctuating tough talk of black listing and institutional and state-sponsored exclusions, Kinoy's enthusiasm was a reminder that struggle and protest are life-long work. Students soon learned that it wasn't only the South that was ambivalent about or hostile to integration. As they read and re-read the papers, they came to see the language of "neighborhood schools," "worries about small children on buses," or "community control" as polite ways for community members to insist on segregated schools. Students quickly saw how fundamentally race was inscribed in the history of our town.

Once the students had created an archivally derived time line of the major segregation and desegregation events, and read and heard the local and national histories, they launched into the interviews. They identified key players from the newspaper articles and then recruited widely for a broad sample of potential interviewees. Early in the fall, a small group of students wrote a letter that appeared in the local newspaper, inviting bus drivers, teachers, students, crossing guards, shopkeepers, and parents who observed or participated in the late 1960s integration struggles to contact the school for an interview. More than 20 interviews were completed across the school year.

With the guidance of both of us and their peers, students prepared themselves for the interview process. They generated the questions to be asked, role played the passive or reticent interviewee and the one who wouldn't stop speaking. We explained that oral history interviews should be designed to elicit personal stories, filled with contradiction, multiple story lines, and layered experiences. We sought variety, not consensus. We were all surprised at the level of sophistication and honesty students brought to the project, evidenced by the tough questions they asked the interviewees: "Did the teachers take out their anger on you because you were 'colored'?" "Did other kids, I mean, White kids, invite you to their house for dinner?" "Were you upset that your parents brought a lawsuit?"

In preparing for the interviews, there was a long and staccato-like conversation about language, in particular whether they should use "colored," "Negro" (the vernacular of the times), "Black," or "African American" in the interviews. One African-American male student asked if it would be appropriate to use a term he relies on to signal endearment and friendship—"Nigger"—seemingly naive about history. The class argued with varied points of view. We decided, ultimately, out of respect for our interviewees, that we wouldn't use "Nigger," but "colored" or "Negro" would be acceptable if the interviewees used that language first.

Later in the year, this conversation was resurrected, this time specifically about the use of "Nigger" or "Nigga," among African American boys and in their music. Ali, the grandson of one of the women who initially brought the lawsuit for desegregation, had just conducted a phone interview with his grandmother about the litigation. Hanging up, he turned to Bernadette and some friends and asked, almost innocently, "You know, given what my grandmother and her friends did, how come we use 'Nigger' so easily, when it was used to put us down?"

Students were, as well, surprised and provoked by some of the interview material. Expecting, for example, stories about discrimination from Whites and solidarity among Blacks, the students asked a number of interviewees who were children in the 1960s, "Were the White children nice to you?" fully expecting a "No." They were surprised to hear from two respondents: "Some of the White children were better friends to me than some of the other Negro children." A tough-going conversation ensued, with students who were White, African American, and biracial asking, "Why would Black children be mad that you were doing well in school, and a cheerleader?" Two African American students admitted that it was "hard to talk about that in front of some of the White kids." Stories of intraracial struggles moved to the surface, sharing the floor with stories of interracial conflicts. An African American teacher from Connecticut, who was visiting Renaissance that day, admitted her discomfort when she listened to a light-skinned respondent recall, "I remember being invited, often, to many White homes for sleep-overs." Recalling her own shunning by White girls in the 1950s, this teacher offered, "Try havin' nappy hair and real dark skin and see if you got invited." This sparked conversations about skin color, "good hair," who gets invited to White sleep-overs, and who doesn't.

And then there were the chilling, recognizable historic revelations about our town that shivered through the class. During an interview with Lydia Davis Barrett, once a child in the Montclair public schools and subsequently director of the Essex County Urban League, students learned the following:

> So we decided to go to the White people's pool to take lessons—boy were they surprised to see us, but they just said, "You sure you're in the right place?" to which we said that we were sure. But what hurt me so, as I approached the pool, is that I realized in the colored people's pool we had to dip our feet in a bucket of disinfectant...no such rule in the White people's pool.

Davis Barrett continued:

> I graduated first in my class, or so I thought, from Glenfield and then I got to the high school and I was getting Ds. I didn't understand it, and my father was mad. He tried to find out what was going on. Was I messing up? Were the teachers racist? And then he discovered that I was first in my class, at least first among the colored children, but we were given a "colored" curriculum at Glenfield. We weren't getting the same rigor, the same courses as the White children, so of course once I got to the high school I was way behind.... My dad wanted to bring a lawsuit but he was a civil servant and they told him if he did, he would lose his job.

Students sat stunned and open-mouthed. Some were disbelieving. Others were familiarly pained.

An important set of pedagogical turns emerged as we realized the unconscious assumptions that infused our work. For instance, when students sympathetically asked some of the children of activists, "Was it difficult being the child of an activist?" they learned that their worries were misguided. We had all assumed the litigation was difficult and embarrassing. We prepared questions that were appropriately sensitive. However, most of the men and women who were intimately involved said the lawsuit was "thrilling." One woman explained, "I knew they [my parents] loved me because they were willing to take up the fight." We had to go back to our interview protocol and reassess the "biases" in all of our questions and search for other buried assumptions.

In interviews with African American and White men and women—educators, parents, activists, then-children in the schools—we heard detailed stories of White resistance to integration, some surprising White support, and the delights and the vulnerabilities of having a "mixed" group of friends. We heard about "colored" support for integration and some class/political tensions within the Black community. We learned about housing segregation that seemed just too hard to undo, so schools became the site for the struggle. There were times we had to challenge ourselves to think about why the schools built in the "Negro" section of town were so well equipped with gyms, equipment, theaters, and music and dance studios, especially compared with the schools in the "White" section of town. And then we realized that the School Board assumed, and they were probably right, that some White people would have to be bribed to put their children on a bus to go to the "other" side of town. Across interviews, it seemed painfully clear that most White children were going to get a good education, integration or not. And that African American students lost opportunities during segregation and then, again, experienced a new kind of racism, and confronted a more veiled segregation through tracking, even after the "victory."

A memorable moment came when students interviewed Dr. Mindy Fullilove. Now a psychiatrist at Columbia-Presbyterian, Dr. Fullilove is the daughter of a civil rights activist from a neighboring town, Orange, New Jersey, who used to "skip to school, as a young child, loving every day." She knew as a child that her father was involved with a civil rights struggle in his town. She didn't know, however, that if he won, she would have to go to school with White children. He won. Dr. Fullilove told the seventh graders, "Integration almost killed me." At that moment we realized that an unspoken, unchallenged bias floated in the room and saturated our interviews: that segregation was bad and integration was good. Unacknowledged were the pain, the loss, and the questionable consequences of integration, especially for African American children, families, and teachers. We spent much time reconsidering how every so-called solution to social injustice brings with it other burdens, other struggles. We realized that African Americans in the Americas can never rest assured that racism has been put in its place. As painful, we saw that racism and White supremacy do not disappear within integration; they merely take on new forms.

But insights never come easy and they don't come to everyone at the same time in the same way. There were significant points of dissension among us for which we, as educators, had to create both room and respect, as well as analysis. For example, Kaelan (a White girl) and Trevor (a biracial boy) argued powerfully and with conviction about how to ask about "teachers" after integration. Kaelan preferred what she thought was a "neutral" question, like, "What were the teachers like after integration?" while Trevor preferred a more directed, even sharply pointed question, "Did the teachers take out their anger on you because you were colored?" We spent a full

Racial Discrimination Called 'Casual Habi

Charles Baskerville, vice president of the Montclair Fair Housing Committee, in a discussion presentation to the Couples Club of First Baptist Church, urged the group to become active participants in the fight against racial discrimination in housing. Declaring that racial discrimination continues to be "the casual habit of many," he called on white citizens of good will to give public testimony to their religious ideals.

"Very little progress is being made nationally, because brotherhood, like good intentions, is easier to verbalize than to realize," he said. Mr. Baskerville instructed those who would help to break down racial barriers in housing, "Be sure that your realtor agrees to advertise your house as an equal housing opportunity. Be sure that it is shown to all who wish to see it." The Fair Housing spokesman noted that the New Jer-

can hurt the neighborhood a the neighbors themselves."

Mr. Baskerville cited t myth of falling proper values, fear of controversy a fear of intermarriage as son as the usual elements in neig borhood concern. Replying comments on the image of t Negro, Mr. Baskerville clared that "the psychologie destruction of the Americ Negro is the darkest spot the image of our nation. T image of the Negro can or be as good as the white s ciety permits. The Neg must be included in go neighborhoods, in jobs, in t best educational opportuniti on the screen and in the new paper ads; in every facet American life an equal par cipant."

The audience of young marrieds from towns in W Essex probed the speaker the matter of establishing be ter relationships with Negro "Negroes are not anxious session discussing the politics of their questions, why Kaelan would want "nice" data and Trevor might want evidence of struggle. Kaelan knew she was looking for some evidence of White adults who fought against racism, and Trevor knew he was looking for evidence of the pain of integration. Both knew if they didn't ask (for the good news or the bad), these memories might never be reported. We asked the question both ways and got wildly different responses. We recognized that how you ask a question affects what you get in response.

A few weeks later, students in the class were asked to describe the project to a newspaper reporter from the *Newark Star Ledger*. Here, too, the students' racialized postures were evident. One White student said, "It was interesting, really, to hear that people in town didn't know the schools were segregated. They didn't know anything was wrong." An African American boy interrupted, "Lots of people knew something was wrong but they didn't know what to do about it." Even at the end of the year, after a dramatic contrast in interviews with White women and African American women activists, as we debriefed, Michelle asked, "What differences did you notice?" A White girl responded, "It was harder for White people to be involved in the protests because they lost friends." At the same moment an African American boy responded, "White people who were involved took all the credit." We analyzed again what the women said and then what we heard. In our analysis we noticed a story within a story: a tale of race, class, and gender gone by and a tale of race, class, and gender in our midst. That is, we spent much time trying to figure out how each of the interviewees and each of us constructs narratives of our lives and our politics, how profoundly our race, class, and gender positions influence what we hear, how we frame and interpret issues of social (in)justice.

Across the year, students came to see that what is taken for granted today in their lives has a long national and local struggle in its shadow. Some went home and asked their parents about going to Montclair High School in the 1960s. Others gathered stories about segregated schools in the South. They started to question their own lunchroom and their future. What's going to happen when we hit high school, will we "split" again by race? Why were some Whites so scared to go to school with Blacks? Why were some Black students so hard on other Black children who were academically achieving? Why were there so few Black educators, even today? As educators, Bernadette and Michelle noticed that there were, and are, conversations still too terrifying to wander into, assumptions too horrifying to challenge, such as: What counts as smart—and is it genetic? What about all those teachers who encouraged some students to believe they were smart and others to believe they were not adequate? What are the peer costs of being academically engaged for African American children? How do we make sense of the racial segregation of special education? What does it mean to be biracial, really part White and part Black, or part Asian and part Black, or part White and part Latino, in this conversation? Why is "basic skills" so segregated? How does social class interact with race and ethnicity in this town, and in this country? Why do people make judgments about me because I am African American and most of my friends are Caucasian? What happens when we have to decide whose music to play at the dance? And ultimately, we all had to reflect on a question we didn't entertain at the beginning of the year: Is integration really better?

For some students, this project simply reiterated a history of struggle that had been their family's history of struggle. It was in their blood, their legacy, discussed over the dinner table. For others it was new and painful, awkward or even embarrassing. White students and educators had to figure out what kind of legacy we brought to the table; African American students and educators had to confront tough evidence of separation, hatred, and denial of opportunity burned into their collective memory; biracial, Asian, and Latino students had to carve out a place for themselves in this history. All students had to assess their own relation to this struggle. No one, of course, wanted to see themselves or their kin as "bad guys," eager to perpetuate unequal racial and class opportunities. But then the conversation turned to what to do if one witnesses unequal or unfair treatment of a student by a teacher, by another classmate, or by a stranger. Simply watch and turn? Intervene? Tell a teacher? Encourage it?

"By just watching," someone remarks, "if we do nothing, then it keeps going on. I mean, we allow it to get worse." And so these young people in the 1990s, the babies of the generation who thought we fixed all this, by year's end began to confront the ongoing politics of race, class, and gender. And to this list they added the politics of "being fat," "having bad clothes," "stuttering," "not being very masculine," "they say I'm gay," "not having a mother," "having big breasts," and, as always, "where we sit in the lunchroom."

Months into the course, three African American boys walking home were stopped by the police. The backpacks of these sixth and seventh graders were searched. Apparently a passerby had called the police and said that a group of boys—one of whom had a gun—were throwing snowballs. Unsuspecting, these boys had stopped to purchase some gum. The police insisted that they stand still to be frisked, and a young White girl from Renaissance, on her way to dance class, saw the confrontation. She had her mother call Dr. Anand immediately because she knew something was wrong. She would not "witness passively."

As it turned out, the boys were fully innocent and the police were asked to come to the school to speak with the school community, including the boys and their parents. Students, parents, and faculty across the school engaged in an analysis of the history, politics, and practices of police harassment of children of color. This incident occurred only 2 days after the Amadou Diallo murder in New York City. Today, students and faculty are organizing a strategy for a delegation of Renaissance students and faculty to visit stores that are "discriminately suspect" of young people. Some students are conducting community-based research in which White and African American students enter a particular store and the "researcher" documents who is followed, who is asked to leave, who is offered help. They are keeping notes—honing their research and activist skills.

Here we are well beyond the years of formal segregation, post-Civil Rights Movement, thriving in a town well known for its embrace of integration. Indeed, Montclair has been recognized by *New Jersey Magazine* as one of the "nation's best towns for multi-racial families." Yet boys of color are still particularly vulnerable to police surveillance and harassment. But what separates this school from most is that here the administration and faculty decided this police search was a school-wide community assault, an issue in need of historic and social analysis, a dynamic to be studied and halted. A White girl witnessed and reported. The three boys and their families were embraced by a school collectively grieving the pain. An African American police officer came to address the school, relating his own experiences of brutality suffered as a youth, at the hands of police officers, noting that that was the moment when he decided to become an officer himself. At Renaissance Middle School, as part of their formal and informal education, young people across racial and ethnic groups, across social class categories and neighborhoods, learn intimately and critically about the scars of exclusion and oppression, historically and today. They learn, too, that research, resistance, and community organizing are an ongoing part of a life educated for social justice.

When we think back to the class, considering pedagogy and engagement, we note an interesting pattern. In the fall, there was, discernibly, uneven participation. African American boys were much more likely to be involved in the classroom conversations than any other demographic "group" in the room: eager to talk, interview, generate questions and probe more fully. While everyone participated to some extent—given the nature of the project, everyone had to generate questions and conduct interviews—initially it seemed toughest for some of the White boys to engage. Understanding discrimination firsthand, or even secondhand from family and friends, was a critical "asset" in this project. Students who had an "eye" for injustice, who had been educated around the dinner table or perhaps had been scrutinized by "mall security" and surveillance, were most ready to do the research and analysis. Over time, however, with practice at interviewing and being interviewed, independent researching, and analyzing transcripts, engagement was much more even. Eventually, whether they were creating questions, conducting interviews, transcribing, writing parts of the book, titling the book, or figuring out the Table of Contents, most students engaged with curiosity and wisdom.

The last morning of the interviewing phase of the project, two women were scheduled for interviews. A White woman in her 60s, a young mother from the 1970s, who fought hard for integration, was followed by an older African American woman, a university professor, who also fought hard, at the same time, as a parent and community member. Each was asked, in seventh-grade dialect, "So, was life better before integration or after?" The first woman, without hesitation, exclaimed, "Much better after! The students go to school together, they have play dates, they are no longer separated." And the second woman explained, after a long pause, "Neither was better. The struggle continues." Students learned that both answers were, in their time and for each of these women, respectively, "true."

"You Can't Give Up the Power of the Struggle":

AN ORAL HISTORY OF SCHOOL DESEGREGATION BY AMERICA'S YOUTH

For African Americans, Brown meant more than the mandate to desegregate public schools. It meant the end of the Plessy v. Ferguson era of officially sanctioned American apartheid. Brown split American history into B.C. and A.D., in which the promise of the Constitution's protection and of full participation in the life of our democracy finally applied to all its citizens. The Supreme Court's decision was one of the sparks that lighted the fires of the civil rights movement. It stands as one of the defining moments in American history.

Theodore Shaw, deputy director-counsel for the NAACP Legal Defense and Educational Fund

George E.C. Hayes, Thurgood Marshall, and James Nabrit celebrate the win of *Brown* v. *Board of Education* on the steps of the U.S. Supreme Court.

IN THIS BOOK WE turn our gaze to the North, to understand how the delicate politics of desegregation played out in a racially diverse, liberal community, just outside New York City, almost 25 years after *Brown*.

Montclair, New Jersey, finally established its current system of racially balanced schools in the 1970s. That is the fact. Depending on whose perspective one accepts, this effort was a result of a court order, progressive mobilization for integration, or the gradual creation of magnet schools to provide families with "choice." The fact is a time in history. What is critical are the varied, often conflicting, perspectives that provide multiple insights into the events preceding, during, and after this process. The real story is the enthusiasm of today's Renaissance School students, some of whom are the children and grandchildren of the participants in this struggle, who investigated their town's past to better understand its present and future.

A Brief Legal Background
Leading to Desegregation

By the 1970s, federal and state courts and legislative bodies had created legal obligations, albeit without providing vehicles for enforcement, for ending school segregation. In order to retain perspective on the work that had to be done, and the victory won in Montclair, it must be recognized that the emphasis of the courts, governments, and the media has always been on the South. Those struggling in the North had to fight, for the most part, without a sympathetic spotlight to use as leverage for their cause.

In the Reconstruction period immediately following the Civil War, three constitutional amendments and a major civil rights act were passed to provide rights to former slaves. Slavery officially ended with the Thirteenth Amendment, ratified in 1865. Almost immediately "Black Codes" were established, severely restricting the rights of African Americans. Congress responded by passing the Civil Rights Act of 1866, which established that former slaves were citizens with equal civil rights and that the federal courts had jurisdiction over state courts in cases involving Blacks.

The Fourteenth Amendment, ratified in 1868, declared that Blacks were both state and U.S. citizens and that no state could compromise the rights of former slaves. The Fourteenth Amendment is the source of the now-famous clause of due process and equal protection for all citizens, which would become the cornerstone for civil rights cases in the twentieth century. As we will see, in Montclair 100 years later desegregation foes tried to use the Fourteenth Amendment to argue that desegregation violated their own due process for equal protection. The Fifteenth Amendment, ratified in 1870, prohibited the federal and state governments from taking away any citizen's right to vote "on account of race, color, or previous condition of servitude."

When northern troops left the South in 1876, these efforts were usurped by the establishment of the so-called Jim Crow laws. These laws created separate and unequal facilities, from rest rooms, to trains, to schools. There was an inevitable collision in 1896 when the United States Supreme Court heard the case of *Plessy* v. *Ferguson*. Plessy, who was seven-eighths White but viewed as Black under the one-drop rule, challenged a law compelling Whites and Blacks to use separate railroad cars. Jim Crow won. The Court ruled that while the Fourteenth Amendment protected citizens from unfair treatment, racial segregation by itself was not necessarily discrimination. The case became the legal foundation for separating the races in all institutions, including schools. Out of this decision came the oxymoronic term, separate but equal.

Until *Brown* v. *Board of Education* in Topeka in 1954, the de facto (segregation by fact) and de jure (segregation by law) realities of segregation were one. In that case, the Supreme Court reversed *Plessy* v. *Ferguson,* concluding that separate but equal is inherently unequal. *Brown* is regarded, properly, as a landmark for integration cases. In that decision the court ruled

> In the field of public education the doctrine of "separate but equal" has no place. Separate educational facilities are inherently unequal. Therefore, we hold that the Plaintiffs and others similarly situated for whom the actions have been brought are, by Reason of segregation complained of, deprived of the equal protection of the laws Guaranteed by the Fourteenth Amendment.

With *Brown*, de jure segregation could no longer be justified. What *Brown* failed to do was provide a mechanism or remedy to dismantle what the Supreme Court considered inherently unequal. De facto segregation was left in place.

In 1955, *Brown* II was decided in order to provide teeth for the original *Brown* and to mandate that districts desegregate with all deliberate speed in plans formulated by federal district courts. However, this decision failed to provide a timetable for action.

While it would be easy to dismiss *Brown* I and II as merely symbolic, it would be wrong. Within a few years, a number of districts began to move toward integration. Indeed, districts in Kansas and Arizona, as well as Washington, DC, and Baltimore, did act with all deliberate speed. Most did not. Prince Edward County in Virginia, for instance, closed its public schools for 5 years rather than desegregate. Only with the strength of another Supreme Court ruling did the system reopen.

Most profoundly, the legal, political, and social grounding of *Brown* I and II is nothing short of historically groundbreaking. These two decisions provided a political justification for federal actions to enforce what was now national law, the legal foundation for more effective court decisions and federal laws in the next two decades, and a strategic organizing tool for the growing Civil Rights Movement.

Members of the *Little Rock Nine*.

In terms of federal action to support *Brown*, Little Rock, Arkansas, is seen as the watershed. On September 24, 1957, 1,000 U.S. Army troops were sent into this city to escort nine African American children into Central High School. Racially conservative President Dwight David Eisenhower referred to his having to send the troops as among his saddest actions as President. Nevertheless, the president declared, "The Supreme Court has spoken and I am sworn to uphold the constitutional processes in this country." Despite his personal philosophy, President Eisenhower believed that *Brown* I and II had changed the law. He felt compelled to enforce it. A shocked North watched on television.

After Little Rock, the stage was set, albeit reluctantly and often belatedly, for federal intervention in southern schools. Backed by the courts, in 1962 James Meredith was led into the University of Mississippi by federal troops ordered there by a foot-dragging President John Kennedy, followed by troops moving aside flamboyant Governor George Wallace in Alabama. An applauding North watched on television.

Forever linked in our national consciousness to *Brown* was the growing Civil Rights Movement. While it is insulting to earlier activists to believe that the movement began after 1954, it would be equally wrong to dismiss the significance of *Brown* as an inspirational rallying point for activism. In 1955 Rosa Parks and Martin Luther King, Jr. emerged on the national scene with the Montgomery bus boycott, which began in 1955 and ended in 1956, when the Supreme Court ruled that segregation on buses was illegal.

The famous 1960s sit-ins began at a Woolworth's lunch counter in North Carolina when the Greensboro Four (first-year college students Franklin McCain, Joseph McNeil, Ezell Blair, Jr., and David Richmond) demanded to be served in 1960. The 1963 March on Washington, DC, with Martin Luther King's I Have a Dream speech, became the inspiration for civil rights and antiwar activism, which would last into the next decade.

President Lyndon B. Johnson forced through Congress the Civil Rights Act of 1964, which barred discrimination based on race, color, creed, national origin, and sex. The Equal Opportunity Commission was created by this law to investigate discrimination complaints against employers. It also prohibited discrimination in public places such as hotels, restaurants, gas stations, stadiums, and swimming pools. This act was supported in the same year by ratification of the Twenty-Fourth Amendment, which outlawed the use of poll taxes—taxes placed specifically on Blacks to keep them from voting.

In 1965 Martin Luther King led a voting rights march from Selma to Montgomery, Alabama. This march pressured President Johnson into passing the Voting Rights Act of 1965, which again banned the use of poll taxes in federal elections. This act also allowed the federal government to send examiners to register Black voters. In addition, it suspended all literacy tests, another arbitrary means of blocking Blacks from voting, in states where more than 50% of the voting-age population had failed to register for the 1964 elections. By the end of 1965 more than 250,000 Blacks, virtually all in the South, had been registered to vote. This act finally made the Fifteenth Amendment of 1870 a reality.

Consistent with media reports of the time and the history books of today, the Civil Rights Movement, including most major court decisions, the Civil Rights Act, federal interventions, and voting rights drives focused on the South. Hundreds of White and Black northerners were the freedom riders who headed South throughout the 1960s to end segregation. The freedom riders struggled hard, were beaten and sometimes murdered, and gained a great deal of success. However, they returned to a North that also was segregated, including Montclair. The story of the struggle to desegregate in the North is a story less well known, and in many ways less complete, than the struggle we learn about when we study the Civil Rights Movement. It is this important story that the students of the Renaissance School have unfolded and can now teach us.

A Brief History of Segregation in Montclair

> Northerners indulge in an extremely dangerous luxury. They seem to feel that because they fought on the right side during the Civil War, and won, they have earned the right merely to deplore what is going on in the South, without taking any responsibility for it; and that they can ignore what is happening in Northern cities because what is happening in Little Rock or Birmingham is "worse." Well in the first place, it is not possible for anyone who has not endured both to know which is "worse."
> James Baldwin, "Fifth Avenue, Uptown: A Letter from Harlem"

Blacks began living in Montclair in significant numbers in the middle of the nineteenth century, primarily as household servants but also as artisans. While some Blacks lived in wealthy households, or at least in the servant quarters where they

The *Greensboro Four* at Woolworth's lunch counter.

worked, an African American community, separate and certainly not equal, began to emerge around the time of the Civil War. Then, as is still the case today, Blacks lived primarily in the southeastern part of the town. In the nineteenth century there was a clear pattern of not selling or renting to Blacks outside of the southern part of town. Like Blacks in nearby Newark, Blacks in Montclair at the turn of the twentieth century competed with Italians for inexpensive housing. Eventually the majority of Italians dispersed throughout the town of Montclair. As we will see, 100 years later, during the height of the local desegregation struggle, little had changed with respect to Black residential patterns.

The segregated and less-than-equal status of Montclair's Blacks permeated policies of housing, education, and worship, ironically even in the Immaculate Conception Church—whose building is where the Renaissance School is currently housed. Seton Hall Professor Elizabeth Milliken, in her pamphlet on the history of the racially mixed Catholic Saint Peter Claver Church in Montclair, reveals the mostly forgotten story of how the Black Catholics who worshiped at Immaculate Conception were excluded from the main space of worship. Milliken (n.d.) quotes Saint Peter Claver parishioner William Cannaday describing why his family left Immaculate Conception in the 1930s:

> We couldn't sit upstairs. We sat downstairs and they had some sort of speaker system so that we could hear mass. We went there for about two months. Finally someone mentioned to my mother "Don't you know that there is a Black

Church on Elmwood Avenue?" and took her to where it was!
And we started going there. (n.p.)

Segregation in Montclair was not restricted to religion and
neighborhood. The *Montclair Times* reported a talk by civil
rights activist Dr. D. C. Rice, pastor-emeritus of Union Baptist
Church. Dr. Rice, who came to Montclair in 1929 as a youngster,
described a community with segregated hospitals, housing, and
theaters, and a segregated school system with all-White teachers. This progressive northern community had a "colored
YMCA," built under the guidance of Charles Bullock in 1926
and now called the Washington Street YMCA; colored churches;
a colored dance hall; and colored barbershops. At the end of his
1983 talk, Dr. Rice sadly noted the lack of progress when he
described the 19 employees of the Township Department of
Revenue and Finance, noting "not a Black face is to be seen
anywhere."

In our interviews, we heard often and painfully these stories
of community and neighborhood segregation. Lydia Davis Barrett, high school student during the early 1960s and later director of the Urban League of Essex County, described Montclair in
the 1950s:

When we were in elementary school, there were Italians and
Blacks in our neighborhood—we were in a poor to working-
class neighborhood here, the fourth ward. There were also a
couple of Jewish kids.

As she grew, however, "difference" became a problem:

I remember one incident in second or third grade. There
were these two girls who I realized, years later, were Jewish,
but I didn't know at the time. They invited me to play with
them, at their house. And I remember when I went, one of
them came out looking a little strange. She looked awkward.
And she said, "Oh, I think we need to play outside." I
thought I heard her mother's voice.

Davis Barrett vividly provided images of interpersonal but also
institutional exclusion throughout town:

Colored kids went to the colored Y. White kids went to the
[Park Street] Y…that was the way we lived. We didn't partic-

ularly question it. But my friend, that year, for reasons I'll never know, said to me, "We should go to the Park Street Y…" and we went home and told our parents…but they let us go up there. And I remember going up there and looking up at this man in the registration window and saying, "May I please have the registration form?" and I remember this man saying to me, "You sure you're in the right place?" And I said, "Yes." And he gave it to me. We signed up and went to the Park Street Y. I realized…one of the profound consequences of racism…I remember being amazed because in the Park Street Y I didn't have to step in a bucket of disinfectant, but we always did at the colored Y. Of course I ended up with a fungus, I believe from the locker room.

Nan Winkler, a White activist and parent in town, also remembers these same divisions.

Geographically, [Montclair] was very segregated with the exception of some very small areas of town.…There were a lot of progressive people here who were eager to see the system integrated and to see life in a different way but there were also a lot of people who were very racist in their attitudes toward life generally and toward the school system in particular.

Race and class intersected in Montclair, as in every other community in the nation, with complex consequences. Particularly because Montclair had a growing Black middle class, "fitting in" was sometimes a problem, as we hear from Dr. Renee Baskerville.

My life before integration was as part of a family that was considered a middle-class family, so that we enjoyed many of the opportunities that everyone enjoyed in the community of Montclair. I had a membership at the library, the art museum, the YWCA. I worked on the Board of the Recreation Department and served on committees of the United Way. The problem was that we [Black people] had been educated, we had been to college, and we realized that education made us seem like outsiders to other Blacks and to Whites.

The Struggle to Integrate Montclair

Throughout the 1950s and early 1960s, if one were to hear the phrase, Civil Rights Movement, the immediate thought would be of the South. After all, this is where the court battles were fought, where the federal troops were sent, and where the freedom riders rode. And, if one were to believe the media, the South was where all the sit-ins, boycotts, and violence were taking place. But if one thought that, one would be mistaken.

Civil rights protests in the North were very real, although far less publicized then or known today. Montclair was no exception. Increasingly vocal in the 1950s and 1960s, most Northern civil rights activities focused on the tightly woven issues of housing and education.* In 1965, the Montclair Fair Housing Committee called 22 homeowners who had put their houses up for sale. Of these owners, only four said they would sell to an African American family. The Fair Housing Committee also interviewed African American buyers. Among these families, it was found that Blacks were told houses in White neighborhoods were off the market when they were not; were not shown houses in White areas by realtors; were told that the owners would not sell to them; and, finally, were told that mortgages would not be given to them for homes in White areas.

Nan Winkler revealed:

> When we looked for a house here, if we asked a realtor a question about an integrated area or an area where African Americans lived, they assured us that there were no African Americans living in that area, which, of course, is exactly what we wanted to know. But we had hoped for a different kind of answer.

Marlene Anderson, an African American woman who was a high-level administrator in the school district, working for the Superintendent, at the same time as she was advisor to the Black Student Union, remembers growing up in Montclair.

> I'm 50 years old, and at 50, I'm still fascinated by seeing so many interracial children and interracial people. When I

---

* The following information was obtained largely from back issues of the *Montclair Times* and the 1964 Community Audit.

grew up in Montclair, it was Black or White. There were no Puerto Ricans . . . there were no Hispanics of any type. There was a Chinese laundry. And a Chinese family. That was it. And if you were anything other than that, you didn't say. . . . Talking about interracial couples, I came from New York with my husband simply because Montclair was that kind of town. We wanted to live here because we felt that this was a place where we would be able to be happy and raise children.

Educator Bernadette Anand tells a similar story of coming to Montclair.

I was living on the Upper East Side. Then we moved to Montclair because I got married and we wanted our children, who were going to be biracial [Indian and White] to grow up in a town that we felt was an integrated town.

Mary Lee Fitzgerald, educator, Superintendent of Schools in Montclair, and Commissioner of Education for the state of New Jersey, remembers her days of moving in.

One of the things I did, because I am White, I bought a house in an all-Black neighborhood, because I . . . can't talk about integration as well if I'm going to live in a White neighborhood. So I wanted to personally try to integrate a neighborhood. And I learned a lot from my neighbors. I was the only White person in about six blocks. And there were old timers who had been in Montclair for a couple of generations. And they were very open to me, which I appreciated. I often thought if this had been reversed, if it was an all-White neighborhood and one Black moved in, I don't know if the neighbors would have been as welcoming as my neighbors were there.

Joe Fortunato, activist lawyer who grew up in Upper Montclair, recounts:

I remember the first time I ever saw a Black youth in Upper Montclair. . . . Maybe he was 6 years old and I was very curious because I had never seen a person like this in Upper Montclair. I began to follow him—the boy—down the street and then began talking to him. And soon a truck came by and . . . an Italian American man who apparently was caring for the boy . . . the boy may have wandered off, and I remem-

ber the man scolding him for running off…perhaps he was thinking that it was something scary for him to be walking the streets of Upper Montclair at the point.

Judy Miller, professor emeritus of Black studies at Seton Hall University, narrates the tense and intimate relation between housing and school segregation.

Kids [would] go to neighborhood schools and the neighborhoods were all-Black so they [would] go to all-Black schools…so, part of the issue that we all got involved in was [the Fair Housing Act] to find a house that you wanted. So that became part of the breakdown of segregation. There were practically no Black people who lived in Upper Montclair. That was our Mason-Dixon line and you didn't cross over that.

By 1968, the Fair Housing Committee revealed that little progress toward integration had been made. Using Black and White testers to find available housing, the Committee established that in areas outside of the southeastern section of Montclair, Blacks were still told there was a waiting list or simply that no housing was available. Whites were shown housing in these areas immediately. Realtors were doing their job in keeping the African American community in the southeastern part of town.

Among the leaders of Montclair's Civil Rights Movement was Charles Baskerville, whose daughter Dr. Renee Baskerville was interviewed by the Renaissance students as a former student who had survived the desegregation struggle to become a pediatrician, and whose grandson, Ali, was one of the Renaissance School students involved in this study. In November 1965, Charles Baskerville, who among other roles served as Chairman of the Montclair Civil Rights Commission, summed up Montclair: "White racial discrimination and Negro racial magnetism have combined to produce the great ghetto we have today."

Later that year, Baskerville, in discussing housing discrimination in Montclair, noted that Montclair had a housing segregation index of 80.3, even higher than Newark's 71.6. The residential patterns provided the justification for a de facto segregated school system, rationalized in the language of "neighborhood schools."

Tensions with the lack of progress toward integration rose throughout the nation and, perhaps not surprisingly, throughout the North in the 1960s; frustration at times erupted into open confrontations, sometimes violence. After a series of what were called disturbances by the *Montclair Times*, George Rice, president of the Montclair NAACP, stated:

> Recent demonstrations are the results of an internal combustion. They are caused by utter frustration. After years of countless humiliations, it is not at all surprising that they occur. (*Montclair Times*, July 27, 1967)

Organizations such as the NAACP, the Fair Housing Committee, the local Civil Rights Commission, and church-led protests pressured the formal and informal institutions of the community to admit that Montclair, not just those distant localities in the South, needed to change morally and structurally. Increasingly, youth in Montclair, as was the case elsewhere throughout the North, were losing their patience with both the White establishment and the traditional Black leadership. At the forum with Mr. Rice, Vincent A. Gill, of the Montclair Civil Rights Commission, noted:

> This near riot in Montclair is local evidence that our town suffers from the same ills that have beset Newark, Nyack, Birmingham and Detroit.... Old leaders have been rejected and new leaders have been chosen from their [young people] ranks. Current events reflect their extreme frustration and a growing determination to pay the ultimate price to motivate change. This was the mood as I sensed it while "holed up" with a group of angry young Negroes on that tense Sunday night, July 16. (*Montclair Times*, July 27, 1967)

This anger rose to the surface in 1968. In July, a few young Blacks broke windows in the southeastern business district of Montclair. While extremely small in scale, this action had a traumatic effect on both the Black and White communities. More significant, that Fall there was a demonstration at the high school. The Black Student Union held a half-day sit-in the cafeteria, with reports of some vandalism and rumors of unprovoked attacks on White students.

The men and women whom we interviewed remembered the power and passion of the demonstration. Renee Baskerville was a student at the time.

The sit-in that I remember was about a guidance counselor in the high school, Mr. Lee. I remember there was some controversy about his job situation...he was Black and his contract had not been renewed. There were questions from the parents in the community [about what had happened]. We all sat in the cafeteria and took over, and it was...[designed] to try to keep Mr. Lee on and trying to get the Board of Education to recognize him and not hold him back because he was Black. There were some tables turned over. The police came in. There was some unrest, but I don't remember any bloodshed....

I can remember it being a warm feeling for me because we [took over the cafeteria]. Martin Luther King was a great influence in those times. And I remember feeling very special and warm inside to be a part of this, which I felt was a peaceful demonstration. I remember sitting there and we were rocking back and forth, singing, "We Shall Not Be Moved." I don't remember it being depressing. I don't remember being frightened by the tables that were overturned. I just remember feeling very important because I knew I was part of something that was hopefully going to bring about positive change and it was a wonderful feeling to be a part of history.

Nan Winkler also remembers this period in history vividly.

The controversy regarding Mr. Lee was as intense as any I remember. It was prolonged and involved numerous community meetings. We lost. His contract was not renewed. He was in touch with the issues and willing to discuss them with his students. No wonder his contract was not renewed.

An equally spirited, although very different, account is narrated by Marlene Anderson, who was working for the Board of Education at that time and was advisor to the students.

It was scary to work for the Board of Education during the protests. You had your moments when you didn't know whether or not, if you made any flares or you were contrary to what the Board felt,...you were going to lose your contract or you may not have your job, or...you had to go elsewhere to work. At that time, the Board of Education was not as liberal as it is now. We did not have as many Blacks in the administration level. So therefore, we had to bite our tongues a little bit as to what our feelings were about the segregation problem that they felt was in town. You didn't know whose toes you were going to step on. You didn't know how many people who had been smiling at you all along were really racially involved.... There weren't that many [Blacks] who stood up for themselves at that time because of the fact that...we didn't have enough Blacks in authority...so if we were going to do something, we were on our own.

The demonstrations were more prominent in the high school...they started with food fights, in the cafeterias, because although we had racial discrimination here, our kids weren't violent—neither the Blacks nor the Whites.... They were just striving to get the attention of the adults. They were striving to get the attention of the Board of Education. They just wanted them to listen...and they weren't so much fighting for integration in Montclair, they were fighting for equal education. They were protesting for equality.

To paraphrase the 1968 Kerner Commission Report on Civil Disorders, by the end of the 1960s Montclair was recognized as divided into two societies, separate and unequal.

Segregation in the Schools in Montclair

Prior to *Brown* v. *Board of Education*, segregation in the South was explicit and legal. This de jure segregation separated children into "White schools" and "colored schools." Not so in the North. Prior to, and for a long time after, *Brown* v. *Board of Education*, de facto segregation existed under the guise of local schools. When necessary, creative gerrymandering—the drawing of neighborhood borders to isolate or protect privileged groups—ensured a segregated school system. Jane Manners in her analysis "Repackaging Segregation: History of the Magnet School System in Montclair, NJ" articulates how a series of "gerrymanded student attendance zones...intentionally separated black and white neighborhoods..."(1998, p. 56). Soon, a pattern in Montclair existed prior to and, more significantly, after the *Brown* v. *Board of Education* decisions.

TABLE 1. Percentage of Minority Students in Montclair Public Schools

School	1947–48	1964–65
Bradford	0	0
Edgemont	0	3
Glenfield	85.4	97
Grove St.	37.4	32
Nishuane	51.2	75
Northeast	0	0
Rand	76.4	84
Southwest	N/A	3
Watchung	1.7	6
Hillside	11.3	36
		34 (Grades 7–8)
Mt. Hebron	0	0
		33 (Grades 7–8)
Montclair High	25	30

That de facto segregation was the rule in Montclair, as demonstrated in Table 1, made it no worse than other northern towns; however, Montclair certainly could not justify claims of moral superiority to the segregated South. In fact, the schools in the southern part of Montclair, Glenfield, Nishuane, and Rand, became more—not less—segregated in the decade after *Brown* v. *Board of Education*.

Nan Winkler reiterates the problem.

We had moved to Montclair in the hopes that there would be a better scene as far as integration was concerned. So it was disturbing that my children were not getting the maximum benefit of an integrated school system....Yet my children did not experience the worst of segregation. Partly because they, in elementary school, were in a school that had at least some African American population, but also because in our personal life, they were part of our group of friends who were quite diverse. So that they were never in a situation which was totally cut off, as White kids....

...But one of the things that disturbed me was when [my children] heard bad comments—and I can recall a particular incident where my son came home from fooling around in the playground after school, there had been some racist comments and he didn't—he was very young—know how to react. It was the beginning of my thinking about the fact that the classroom really needed to deal with issues, so that the children...learned how to talk about it with one another.

Lydia Davis Barrett details the problem and the resistance.

About integration? Well I guess you could say that during elementary through junior high school, the situation was that nobody felt there was a situation...there was only one Black teacher and she happened to be an outstanding teacher. I was fortunate enough to have her, Mabel Hudson, when I was in fourth through sixth grade. By the time I got to junior high school at Glenfield, there was a second Black teacher—Daisy Douglas—I was one of her worst students...but she was gracious enough not to acknowledge that. There was no mandate to have curriculum that integrated the African American experience...but there was a mandate to study the Native American experience. And I remember wondering why Mabel Hudson went into such depth and detail. She somehow, I guess, felt that she could teach us [the histories of] people of color even though she wasn't really free to teach us African American history.

In a parallel voice, Renee Baskerville explains:

I grew up in the south end of Montclair and I remember then that the schools were very segregated. And all the kids in my class were Negroes...I am trying to keep with the language of time...[but] I remember having mostly White teachers.

In contrast, Joe Fortunato remembers:

TABLE 2. Percentage of Black and Latino Students Attending Schools Where at Least 90% of the Students Are Minorities

BLACK STUDENTS			LATINO STUDENTS		
Rank	State	Percent	Rank	State	Percent
1	Michigan	64.0	1	New York	58.8
2	Illinois	60.3	2	Texas	45.7
3	New York	60.3	3	California	42.2
4	New Jersey	51.3	4	New Jersey	40.7
5	Maryland	49.7	5	Illinois	37.8
6	Pennsylvania	46.7	6	Connecticut	31.3
7	Alabama	43.1	7	Florida	29.2
8	Mississippi	41.2	8	Pennsylvania	26.5
9	Tennessee	40.8	9	Arizona	22.7
10	Louisiana	40.3	10	New Mexico	22.1

Source: *The Star Ledger*, July 18, 2001

Starting kindergarten in Mt. Hebron and then junior high ... my kindergarten class was entirely White and it remained that way through the sixth grade for me...there was one Jewish student, and he was a very distinct minority. He was looked at as being different because he had a different religion, perhaps he didn't celebrate Christmas. But the concept of going to school with Black students just didn't occur to us. This wasn't part of our reality.

Montclair's history is a familiar, if unspoken, one. It is a history of segregation of schools, housing, and worship—a segregation that this community, and the northeast, are still coming to grips with. At the end of the twentieth century the lack of progress toward residential integration remained pronounced in the most densely populated northeastern states. Montclair is no exception. It is still predominantly Black in the southeastern part of town and still predominantly White in the northern area known as Upper Montclair.

As Table 2 illustrates, New Jersey, and neighboring New York and Pennsylvania are among the most segregated states. In a

1999 national study conducted by Gary Orfield and John T. Yun, and updated in 2001, New Jersey and New York consistently rank among the top ten most segregated school systems. Orfield and Yun conclude that

> Large and increasing numbers of African-American and Latino students are enrolled in suburban schools, but serious segregation [characterizes] these communities...[and] all racial groups except whites experience considerable diversity in their schools but whites are remaining in overwhelmingly white schools even in regions with very large non-white enrollments. (1999, p. 1–2)

In 2001, Orfield is cited in the *Star Ledger.*

> New Jersey is like much of the Northeast, where the pattern of segregation is high and getting slightly worse,... Actually, it has been so segregated in these states that it is hard for them to get much worse. (Mooney, 2001)

Civil rights and educational activist Walter Lack recounts his days on the Civil Rights Commission, confronting issues of race and class discrimination in schools and in housing.

Three-Year Te

Mayor Mary V. Mochary yesterday said she has re-appointed Walter A. Lack of Lorraine Avenue and Kenneth Miscia of Park St. to 3-year terms on the Board of Education.

With the reorganization of the school board at its annual meeting next month, Mr. Lack will commence his second full term, while Mr. Miscia, who was appointed last year to complete an unexpired term, will begin his first full term.

Mr. Lack was appointed to the board in February of 1978.

A partner in Lack & Lack, certified public accountants, New York, since 1954, he received his CPA certificate in 1953 and is a member of the New York Society of CPAs.

Within the community, Mr. Lack has served as chairman of the education committee of the Greater Montclair Urban Coalition which studied the proposed school desegrega-

(Continued on Page 11)

WALTER A. LACK

> *My sense is that a large part of the problem is also related to class. I think that people aren't paying enough attention to the economic class aspect of this.... But in some instances, we adults tend to put [racism] on you [students]. So I don't think it's real shocking that there's racial segregation even today. New Jersey is [after all] the second and fourth most racially segregated—by schools and housing—according to the 1990s census. So if the cafeteria is segregated, that's a reflection of what's going on in our state. And that's promulgated by adults.*

As Jane Manners details, in the late nineteenth century, before immigrant Italians were accepted by the rest of the White community, both Black and Italian children who attended public schools were assigned to the Cedar Street School (later renamed Nishuane) in the southern part of town. Erected in 1887, this school was designed by the Board of Education to ensure that these two groups would not attend school with "White" students. In 1896 the Maple Street School (now called Glenfield) was erected in the southeastern part of town to further ensure that Black and Italian children would remain in their neighborhood. Both schools were K–9. Once Italians began moving out of the southern part of town, Nishuane and Glenfield became increasingly "colored" schools.

After ninth grade, these students would join the rest of the town in a single high school. However, by the time they arrived at the high school, the inferior quality of their feeder schools made tracking by race easily justifiable. And tracking, in small northern municipalities such as Montclair that had only one high school, became another means of de facto segregation within a building.

Things could have been complicated for Montclair since there was a small, but wealthy, White community in the southwestern part of town. By the late 1940s, the Board was faced with the possibility of sending White students from the southwestern part of town to the predominantly Black Nishuane and Glenfield schools. The Board came up with another idea—create another neighborhood school. In 1949 the Board converted a former mansion in the southwestern part of town into the Southwest School. Table 1 on page 28 illustrates just how effective this policy of de facto versus de jure segregation remained into the 1960s, with Southwest 97% White and Glenfield 97% Black. In large part, the creation of Southwest School, in combination with the exodus of White families, explains the increase in segregation between the late 1940s and mid-1960s.

The Fight for Desegregation in the Schools*

...The [State] Commissioner [of Education] directs the Montclair Board of Education to formulate a plan which will effectively achieve the goal of racial dispersal enunciated by the Courts as the law of New Jersey.
                    Commissioner of Education, November 8, 1967

In Montclair it was a long, uphill climb from *Brown* v. *Board of Education* in 1954 to the final implementation of a desegregation plan in the late 1970s—longer than the desegregation struggles in Little Rock, Birmingham, and throughout the South.

The secret, as the 1960s began, was not that Montclair had segregated schools. That was explicit and rationalized by neighborhood boundaries. The secret, although hindsight does not allow it to be a surprise, was that the separate schools were not equal. As many of the interviewees told the Renaissance students, the predominantly Black schools were not fully educating their students, did not have the same resources or curricula as the White schools, and, most significant, were not educating toward high expectations for their students.

Public protests over school segregation in Montclair began in 1961. Parents at Glenfield Junior High School, with the local NAACP, challenged then Superintendent Clarence Hinchey and the Board of Education over "unequal and inferior" educational opportunities. The June 29, 1961 *Montclair Times* reported a heated 5-hour meeting with the Board of Education at which parents demanded establishment of a citizen's advisory committee to study elementary and junior high schools across Montclair. The parents also demanded an immediate redistricting of school boundaries.

One of the leaders of the parents was Glenfield PTA President Harris Davis. Davis's daughter—Lydia Davis Barrett, who as an adult was director of the Urban League of Essex County—went from straight As at Glenfield to Ds at the high school.

> Here I was, this great big honor student from Glenfield—which was mostly Black—and I failed the first essay in Montclair High. I was getting similar mediocre grades in algebra. (Mays, 1998, p. 52)

Davis, after concluding that these poor grades were the result of his daughter's inadequate preparation rather than failure to adjust to high school, organized other parents into a Parents' Emergency Committee. Lydia Davis Barrett remembers:

---

*This section is derived primarily from information from the commissioner of Education's decisions, court records, the *Montclair Times*, various Board of Education documents, and Jane Manners's article in *Race Traitor*, 1998, Volume 8.

> What my father discovered is that we weren't getting the
> same content as kids in the White schools...we were
> getting old, outdated textbooks from White schools.
> There were low expectations. (Mays, 1988, p. 52)

Working with the NAACP, the Emergency Committee found

> disparities similar to those found in "separate but equal"
> systems in the South. The schools in Montclair's white
> neighborhoods had newer supplies, more rigorous curricula,
> better facilities and more experienced teachers....The pre-
> dominantly white schools received new textbooks and furni-
> ture on a regular basis, while Glenfield had to be content
> with hand-me-downs.... White schools had new science lab-
> oratories, extensive library, and fully-equipped gymnasiums
> and cafeterias....Finally Glenfield's teaching staff did not
> have the same credentials as those in other schools. (Man-
> ners, 1998, pp. 59–60)

Lydia Davis Barrett tells this story:

> *When I went to Glenfield, I won a lot of awards for academ-*
> *ics.... My parents were both college graduates so you had to*
> *sign up for whatever kind of program you wanted at the*
> *high school. And I signed up for the college prep program.*
> *When I went to pick up my schedule, I had cooking as a*
> *major and sewing as a minor...but I had signed up for col-*
> *lege prep which meant I needed 5 days of language, math,*
> *and English.... My father had to leave his job for a day. In*
> *those days fathers didn't leave their jobs for a day to go to*
> *school. But he had to leave his job and go up to that high*
> *school in order to make them give me back the college prep*
> *program. [When I started getting low grades at the high*
> *school], my father made a fuss...only to learn that although*
> *I graduated top of my class at Glenfield, I had been receiving*
> *the curriculum for students who were [classified as] Negro.*

In this struggle, the Davis family—and the Black community—
learned that students were receiving very different curricula,
supplies, and facilities based simply on race.

   Following a brief community boycott of Glenfield, at the
beginning of the 1961–62 school year, Superintendent Hinchey
and the Board made vague promises to study the situation, as
well as half-hearted, ineffective gestures toward creating desegre-

gation plans. However, every attempt to ease the segregation situation was met with opposition from White parents who formed organizations such as the Committee for Neighborhood Schools. These parents, defending the "neighborhood school" concept, explained that it would be inappropriate to bus children beyond their neighborhoods. They argued that busing would tire their children out and thus would be educationally unfounded, ignoring the fact that neighborhood segregation and creative gerrymandering had created the White and Black neighborhoods in the first place.

As we learned from Nan Winkler, there was another historical force—one easily overlooked in history.

> There was a group of African American parents (and supporters) in Montclair, as throughout the country, who [also] believed that integration was not the solution to inequities in education. Some believed that as long as White people were in control, making all of the decisions, the interests of Black children would not be served. They questioned the sensitivity of White people to the culture and history of the Black community. They understood that the expectations for their children would remain low. These parents supported the concept of "community control," wherein the community would have the power to make decisions regarding the education of their children. Many of their fears have been borne out. We continue to struggle with these issues.

In 1962 the Committee for Neighborhood Schools went to court, claiming that a Board of Education plan to create limited integration at Mt. Hebron denied their own White children equal protection of rights guaranteed under the Fourteenth Amendment. In May 1964, the New Jersey Supreme Court ruled against the Committee for Neighborhood Schools, stating that the Board could indeed use race as a factor in school assignments. The Court also declared that the Fourteenth Amendment rights of the Mt. Hebron students were not violated.

Later in 1964 Superintendent Hinchey left the district and was replaced by Robert Blanchard. Blanchard and the Board of Education failed to take advantage of the New Jersey Supreme Court ruling beyond annually offering half-hearted plans for desegregation. These plans were unacceptable to the pro-integration forces, for not going far enough, and equally unacceptable to the anti-busing constituency, which continued to rationalize segregation using the concept of neighborhood schools.

Meanwhile, within the schools, Marlene Anderson tells us:

> *At the time I went to Montclair High School, in the early 1960s, I had never heard of a Black college. I was never even called into the guidance office to be evaluated to go to college. I wasn't geared toward that direction. We didn't have any Black guidance counselors.... Some classes had all Black students. We actually had classes that were segregated.... The Black Student Union, eventually, was formed to fight for the rights of all the students in Montclair. They were trying to make it better for all the kids.*

Frustrated by the lack of progress, in 1966 Black parents petitioned the New Jersey Commissioner of Education. These parents accused the Montclair Board of Education of failing to seriously and adequately desegregate Montclair schools. The suit claimed that the Board's inaction led to a

> denial of their right to equal educational opportunity and they asked that the Board of Education be directed to take positive steps, and to employ fair and impartial standards, to eliminate all aspects of racial segregation and discrimination under its jurisdiction.

On November 8, 1967, the Commissioner recognized in his ruling that the Board had made some plans to desegregate, particularly by considering (1) pairing schools at opposite ends of the town and cross-busing, or (2) closing two schools at the southern sector of the town. The latter plan would recreate the space thus abandoned by construction of new schools or additions to existing schools in the northern sector, and transport the pupils displaced to the new facilities. However, the Commissioner noted that the Board itself had rejected these plans as unworkable. While rejecting the Black parents' contention that the Board failed to recognize the effects of discrimination, the Commissioner directed the Board to implement a complete correction of racial imbalance in its school system.

Renee Baskerville, whose parents were pioneers in the litigation, remembers with great pride this moment in her childhood.

*I don't remember the particulars of what was said or any-
thing like that. But it was a very special time for me,
because I was watching my parents fight for something and
was watching them be dedicated. I was so proud of my parents.*

Parallel to *Brown* v. *Board of Education*, the 1967 ruling by
the Commissioner led to neither immediate nor full implementation. It certainly was a legal victory; however, it would take a
long time to reach fruition. While there was much resistance,
there was also much organizing by parents—mostly Black, but
some multiracial coalitions also began to emerge. Judy Miller
recalls:

*We had meetings trying to find out what it was we should
do...we weren't always in agreement. But we would come to
a consensus after a great deal of talking and examining
what might be best. It wasn't just all Black people. We had a
number of White people who worked with us, and who were
courageous in what they were doing. Sometimes they
received much more overt criticism.... I remember on the
picket lines, men would drive up in a car and they would
yell at us and the children. But a lot of the abuse was
focused on some of the White women doing marches and it
was constant. But it was exhilarating because we were
fighting for integration, which was much more than just
putting Black kids with White kids. The White kids also
received better education, more supplies, a more rigorous
curriculum, more qualified teachers. We were thrilled with
the possibilities.*

Joan Smith, a White parent who was involved in the early struggles for integration, also remembers the power of the meetings
and the strength of parents coming together across race lines to
fight for social justice.

*I think that there was what they called de facto segregation,
which means that in fact they separated some neighborhoods where it was more highly one race or another, and
had them go to those schools.... [Nevertheless] I have to tell
you, there were a lot of wonderful friendships forged between
the races in those years. Between African Americans and*

Caucasian people in the community. There were some won-
derful side benefits of working for this integration
plan…realizing that some of these other parents were poets,
writers…getting to know them as individuals, not just over
the PTA table.

The Board of Education responded with a so-called 5-3-4 Plan, which involved moving Black students in grades 1–4 from Rand School in the south to Watchung and Edgemont Schools in the north; moving White students in the fifth and sixth grades from Watchung and Edgemont to Rand; and placing White fifth- and sixth-grade students from Southwest School in programs in Nishuane School. While this plan did lead to more racial balance, it failed to satisfy the criteria established by the Montclair NAACP and the State Commissioner of Education. The latter ruled on August 19, 1968, that the 5-3-4 Plan proposed by the Board of Education was insufficient and therefore unacceptable. The Commissioner again did not provide either an acceptable remedy or an acceptable time for the Board to act.

One outcome of the 5-3-4 Plan was the establishment of what would become the foundation for Montclair magnet schools. To make Nishuane and Rand more acceptable to White parents, the Board added exciting educational programs. While the Commissioner's ruling negated the 5-3-4 Plan, the notion of the attractive themes for each school would become the foundation for the system that eventually was accepted.

After the Commissioner's rejection of the 5-3-4 Plan, pro-integration forces pushed the Board for a more meaningful desegregation plan. The Committee for Neighborhood Schools, and its successors, resisted all such moves. As Nan Winkler remarked:

People were not saying what they really believed. I mean,
nobody said, "We're against integration." They said things
like, "We're against this change because children have to go
further away from their homes." Or "This is complicated."
Or "There are too many changes." But people did not admit
to being against integration.

It was in September 1968 that a student protest was ignited at the high school. The *Montclair Times* of October 3, 1968, describes

[an] intolerable situation at Montclair High School [in which] the Black Student Union, some 500 strong, decided on a sit-down demonstration.... The high school has been plagued with demonstrations, physical attacks by Negro students upon White students and conditions in the high school not conducive to the democratic process.... Everyone in the community, Negroes and Whites, have much at stake in this critical situation and already many White families, fearful of attacks upon their children, are considering withdrawing them from the high school and moving or sending them to private schools. Montclair can ill afford such a movement, for it wouldn't take long for our schools to become predominantly Negro and the community a ghost town.

The Board as a whole, like the newspaper, often reflected the sentiments of the more elite and White segments of town. The Board, as a body, was not in favor of moving with any deliberate speed. Judy Miller remembers:

I was the first African American president of the PTA council that brought together all the PTAs in town. On the day of the meeting, I got a call that there was trouble in town...one of the first fights in the school and the parents were incensed and they demanded some meetings. The only meeting that was happening in education at that point was our [integrated] parent/teacher council meetings. So we met in the Superintendent's office because we were going to have to go to Hillside to meet 700 parents who were irate about what was happening between Black and White kids...they were furious. It was a meeting that I'll never for-

Vol. XCI, No. 26

Second Class Postage
Paid at Montclair, N. J.

NAACP Attacks School Conditions

'Unequal' Glenfield Opportunities Scored – Redistricting Sought – Taylor to Head Study Unit.

Representatives of the Montclair Branch of the National Association for the Advancement of Colored People joined a group of Glenfield Junior High School parents and others to demand on Tuesday night that the Board of Education take immediate steps to improve "unequal and inferior" educational opportunities afforded the 185 students enrolled there.

For three hours, they criticized school officials for lack of action in the past, for present plans to establish a citizens advisory committee to study on a town-wide basis elementary and junior high school educational facilities and for failure to make an immediate redistricting of school boundaries enabling Glenfield students to attend other schools by the opening of the school year in September.

Five-Hour Session

By the time the five-hour Board session had drawn to a close which found Board opponents as ready to seek information, ask questions and criticize policies as they had been at the start, the announcement of the selection of a committee chairman had all but been forgotten.

Board President Mrs. Helen K. Halligan revealed that former Town Commissioner Philip B. Taylor of 80 Norwood Ave., Upper Montclair, a consulting engineer, who served during the Eisenhower Ad-

Additions, New Plaza Proposed

Forest St., Orange Rd. Valley Rd. Sites Involved.

Development of a new parking plaza on Forest St., near Glenridge Ave., and substantial additions *get…parents were yelling…by the time we got near the end of it, people were calmer.*

It was at that meeting, as reported in the *Montclair Times*, that Irving Winkler saw "the real problem…as naked, unabashed White racism."

Board of Education, 1968 by Irv Winkler

I have three children in our school system and I attended the Town Commission meeting at this school last week which dealt with the current situation in our High School.

It is high time now that someone stood up and told it as it is, characterizing the real problem by its right name—i.e. pure, simple, naked, unabashed white racism—some of it subtle, most about as subtle as the main address at a George Wallace rally. I am both appalled and sick to my stomach at the expression and display of bigotry which pervaded that meeting.

What has our fair town in such an uproar? Several hundred black students join together to develop an organizational form which they apparently felt was necessary to express their particular problems and needs; special problems which result from a very special oppression—a systematic, all encompassing, humiliating oppression which all black people, and particularly black youth, have been subjected to for over two hundred years. We are incensed that they no longer eagerly reach out to grab at some noble white hand, which time and time again has clenched into a steel fist—only to beat them into the ground in a thousand insidious ways. We are outraged with righteous indignation that black youth in our community have come to the conclusion that they must now find their own way, develop their own organizational forms under their own leadership if there is to be any meaningful progress or change.

To those who suddenly lament this polarization of the black community, but who have nothing to say about the lily white polarization that has for decades dominated every aspect of life in this town, not withstanding its racial tokenism; to those who are looking under beds for "outside" black agitators, I for one say thank God these kids have the courage, wisdom and guts to stand up and be counted, to say "What was once good enough, is good enough no longer!" To those who say, "It was never like this when I went to Montclair High where some of my best friends were Negroes," I say we are way behind the times in Montclair. Even the smart bigots quit playing that jazz years ago.

I bring news for my white brothers. The fact is the day is long, long gone, like it or not, when white people could determine who the black leadership should be, or what "Black organizational forms" should be, or what black values should be, or what black demands and aspirations should be—and most particularly, what black tactics in the quest for full freedom now should be. Neither are black people going to be divided or diverted and led down harmless paths by false friends; or intimidated by expulsions, threats, or billy clubs, here in Montclair or anywhere else. The record should be abundantly clear on that score by now!

As a white man I am not here to defend black youth, who need no defense from me. I am here, however, to defend the interests of my own children who attend Montclair schools. I submit that it is no accident that, by and large, the same forces who are now calling for the heads of the school administration, who are spreading the racist rumors, who seek to make political capital from this situation and wreck the preferred plan, who are pushing the law and order bit—are the very same forces who attack every school budget, who organize the "NO" votes in every referendum that determines the quality of our schools and the education which our children shall receive.

These remarks, however, should by no means be taken as approval of the Board or of the latest actions of Drs. Blanchard and Fish. Some of their recent decisions show questionable sensitivity indeed to the special needs of black youth, whose right to organization and recognition are essential to the very life of the democratic process in our school system.

First rate, quality education is as indivisible as freedom itself; just as the targets of bigotry and discrimination are never limited to one racial, religious or national group.

I have every confidence that all of our children, black and white, can resolve this question as they will resolve many of the decisive questions of our time which our own generation has bungled. It is some of the parents and certainly the bigoted troublemakers who constitute the real problem.

And so the Board worked out several more plans. In 1970, one such plan, which involved turning Mt. Hebron and Hillside into integrated middle schools, was rejected by the voters. The following September an interim plan was put into place. This plan left the segregated elementary schools in place and created three middle schools with some integration. Black students would be sent to White schools, but not the reverse. Needless to say, this interim plan was rejected by the State Commissioner of Education.

Michael Johnson, who was leader of the Black Student Union, remembers these early days of one-way desegregation.

> The first stage of desegregation came when Glenfield was closed and each of the Glenfield students was bused to one of the other junior high schools. Thus segregation remained in the K to sixth-grade schools. This plan continued for a few years when they … made Montclair High School a 9–12 program. Now there were only two junior high schools and the entire system was desegregated—but not integrated—7–12. So desegregation was gradual. . . .
>
> It should be kept in mind that desegregation and integration were not necessarily the same thing. As a child, when I lived in the Glenfield area it was a somewhat contained Black community which I imagine continues to a certain degree. The school desegregation movement swept across the country during this period and as a youngster I recognized it as a positive change, though I questioned, along with others, the validity of the assumption that there could not be "excellent" all-Black schools. Thus I had this ambivalence about the School Board's decision which was aggravated by the fact that the burden of the early busing fell on the Black students.

Parent Helen Newhouse remembers the plans and the associated rumors.

> When integration first happened, they struggled for many years to find the right way to do it. . . . What I particularly remember was they transferred a White fifth grade from Bradford to Glenfield and vice versa. . . . Black children were being brought to Mt. Hebron and White children were brought, I think, to Hillside. . . . I remember hearing one rumor that was going around among the children, "Do you know they found a girl's skeleton in Mt. Hebron? You know, DEAD BODIES!"

Educator Frank Rennie discussed some of the political maneuvering of the times.

Frank Rennie

*I don't want to blame the
conflict on the Board of Education,
because the town clearly was not wild about going
into any kind of integration program. It seemed to me they
were just not ready to say, "We're going to bus students
around. We're going to change this." The south end of town
was predominantly Black. Other parts were predominantly
White. So they tried this. It lasted for 2 years until everyone
saw the folly [of moving just a few students]. It was
artificial...it wasn't real because integration didn't start in
the first grade or kindergarten where it should. It was flaunt-
ing...the law said you had to integrate the school, not each
grade. Integration wasn't a choice on the part of the parents.
It was something the Board of Education could do. It upset a
lot of people in town.... There were what we call contentious
meetings because people—and I say it was primarily
Whites—did not want to give up their right to send their kid
to a neighborhood school. That was their pitch. You lived,
you bought a home in one part of town. The more expensive
homes were in the upper part of town. So you bought a home
two blocks away and it was practical, "Oh, my kids are
going to walk to school." And then somebody tells you, "You
can't send your kids to this school. We're going to bus you to
the other end of town."*

Joan Smith, a White parent involved in the PTA and now a disability rights activist, remembers that she, and a group of other
PTA mothers, were very concerned.

We Still Have A Dream

1963
1983

JOBS

PEACE

FREEDOM

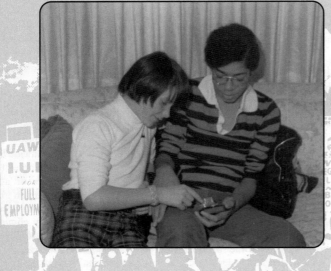

AUGUST 27, 1983 ☆ LINCOLN MEMORIAL ☆ WASHINGTON, D.C.

KEEPING THE STRUGGLE ALIVE

There were people in Montclair who really fought hard for what they believed was the right thing to do for kids. I happen to be one of that group of PTA women. The issue was busing versus neighborhood schools. The Board of Ed tried to convince people that busing was the way to go…it didn't matter what happened on the other end of the bus line, as long as your education was exciting. And a lot of people believed that was true. They believed that all kids in this town were going to get a more equal educational experience, and a better social experience…and a more diverse community. We got tired of listening to all the arguments that went back and forth. We said, "You know what? Let's make an appointment with the Commissioner of Education."

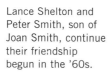

Lance Shelton and Peter Smith, son of Joan Smith, continue their friendship begun in the '60s.

We were a group of PTA parents…we made an appointment with the Commissioner of Education and we went to Trenton. We realized that Montclair was really in noncompliance with the law, that we had been given an order to desegregate our schools and we were tossing the ball all around town. And so we came back and I remember the Montclair Times *had a big spread on the front about* PTA PARENTS GO

TO TRENTON. We felt that [the lawsuit] was just one more step to having the Board of Education recognize the need for a [system of] education that would be open to all children.... But I can remember very heated arguments at PTA sessions and town sessions. Very heated arguments. And sides were taken and racial slurs were made. There were some very unkind remarks. It was a very, very hot issue.

Montclair High School and Harvard University graduate, Jane Manners describes this historic period as follows:

There had been attempts to desegregate the schools for 5 years...and nothing had really happened. They started busing the Glenfield students who were mostly Black to the White middle school, so there was some integration, but it certainly wasn't wholesale. So the Black parents said, "You haven't integrated our schools. The Black students are still getting inferior educations. They are getting the worst supplies...we want integration; we want equal opportunity for student education."... But a lot of the White parents didn't want to send their children on a bus. It's very interesting the words these White parents used to fight these busing proposals. They said they didn't want to send their kids on a bus across town...when they had a perfectly good school 5 minutes away, could roll out of the bed in the morning and walk to school.... And that was...the reason they said that they were all opposed to this busing measure—and they called it forced busing.... [But] there was an interesting law that passed at this time called the Fair Busing Act...which meant that anyone in town should have the same opportunity to take a bus to school if they wanted to...most of the kids who took these buses under the Fair Busing Act were White kids going to private schools.

In February 1972 the Board of Education approved what became known as the "Plan of Action" involving two-way busing. Pushed by new Superintendent of Schools James Adams, this comprehensive plan covered elementary as well as middle school children. Anti-integration forces, who had tolerated, barely, the busing of Black middle school children to White schools, now organized under the banner of a group called Better Education for All Montclair (BEAM). As with its predecessor, the Committee for Neighborhood Schools, BEAM argued that busing was educationally unsound and would lead to a decline in educational quality.

BEAM and other opponents successfully supported anti-busing candidates for the Town Commission in the May 1972 elections. As a result, the Commission increased the number who served on the Board of Education from five to seven and reduced their length of service from 5 to 3 years. In his September 1972 *A Plan of Action*, Superintendent James Adams proposed that "each youngster will attend his neighborhood school for four years...for example, Nishuane's second graders will be assigned to Edgemont and Bradford, while Hillside and Grove second graders will be assigned to Northeast and Glenfield. This assignment of second graders will bring about racial balance at that level."

In shared spirit with then-student Michael Johnson, educator Frank Rennie reflects on this period of history:

> *By the time '72 came around, it was clear that the Board of Education was not moving very swiftly to integrate the schools. It was clear nothing was going to happen unless somebody made it happen. So the Superintendent decided to devise a plan where they would gently go into integration of the schools by taking one class, just one grade, out of the Black school and moving those students into an all-White school, to Northeast, for example. And move the kids from Northeast someplace else to integrate that school.... We had large meetings at Hillside. That auditorium was filled because they had to come up with another and a better plan. There was no other way except to bus kids.... People weren't going to move from one section of town to another.*

Bernadette Anand recalls overhearing a conversation about this time in a neighborhood coffee shop.

> *My husband and I sat down for breakfast one morning. There were all White people sitting at the counter. I remember that there was this one woman really upset about the integration plan. They were saying, "What do they want to do here?" "They want to ruin our town and they want to shove kids in." "I'll be damned...if my daughter is going to go to that school over there and I am going to put her on a*

bus." "Why can't I have a neighborhood school?" My hus-
band and I looked down at the end of the counter...and
they sort of stopped.

Marlene Anderson comments on the same period.

I worked at the school system for the Board of
Education...it was strange to see a town like Montclair actu-
ally involved in racial discrimination because, when I was
coming up in this town, it did not exist in the open...it was
probably there, but it was not presented to us and it was not
exploited.

By 1974 anti-busing forces had full control of the Board. At the
end of 1974 Adams left and was replaced by Walter Marks as
Superintendent of Schools.

In September 1975, this anti-busing Board replaced the *Plan
of Action* with a "Freedom of Choice" policy. Parents now could
avoid having their children bused to the school selected by the
Board if their choices did not lead to racial imbalance. Frank
Rennie explained:

A group of predominantly White parents got together and
they said, "If we're going to have to send our kids to another
school because they have to be integrated, we want to choose
the school that these children go to." It was called "freedom
of choice." And that word has remained today....It saved the
community because they hammered out agreements to make
particular schools a freedom of choice in the magnet
approach...meaning that particular schools would be made
attractive to parents.

This Board approved all requests for choice even though
some, indeed, created further imbalance. Rennie continued,
"But at the time, the policy was implemented in ways that
undermined integration."

In July 1975, the State Commissioner rejected Freedom of
Choice alone as an acceptable plan for desegregation. Freedom
without balance was not a solution to racial segregation. Now
the Commissioner was much more direct with the Board. He
ordered the Board to create a plan in which every school in the
district would reflect the 60% White/40% Black ratio of the
district.

In February 1976, Superintendent Marks was caught between the State Commissioner and conflicting constituencies who were passionately for, or against, busing to create integration. In April, the Superintendent presented five alternate plans to the Board of Education. The plans ranged from the "blue" plan, which called for the closing of five elementary schools and increased busing, to two "red" plans, which called for the cessation of all busing for integration. There were also a "gold" and a "green" plan. These plans would mandate limited busing; however, both emphasized the magnet school alternative. In theory, each school under the "gold" and "green" plans would be so attractive based on its specific theme that for most parents, that is, White parents, busing would be not only digestible but desirable.

In April 1976, the Board shocked Superintendent Marks and voted 4–3 for a modified "red" plan, even though this plan clearly would not be acceptable to the State Commissioner and possibly would cost Montclair substantial federal and state aid. Under this plan, all elementary schools would remain open and all mandatory busing for integration would end. The only policy that the district would offer for integration would be magnet schools based on the foundation of attractive themes.

Within a month, Black parents staged a sit-in at the Board, protesting the adoption of this new "red" plan. Superintendent Marks was supportive of the demonstrators, refusing to have them removed. The Board, recognizing the impending loss of more than $2,000,000 in aid and the strength of the State Commissioner's order, conceded and voted to restore the *Plan of Action* for the 1976–77 year. Finally in June 1976, the Board voted 6–1 for a new "green" plan for implementation in the 1977–78 school year for the schools. This plan called for incorporation of magnet schools and, like the "red" plan, did not directly call for mandatory busing for racial balance. However, distancing itself from the "red" plans, the new "green" plan required at least 25% "minority students" in each of the K–9 schools.

The 1976–77 school year was spent selling the magnet plan to the community, which meant largely the White community. Attractive themes for two magnet schools, at Nishuane and Hillside, were developed. These schools, which had been predominantly African American, became magnets for "gifted and talented" children. What White parent would deny a child this option?

Many resources were added in order to encourage White parents to send their children "south." Indeed, a number of astute seventh-grade interviewers asked: "Why did they have to bribe White parents to send their kids to our schools—but not bribe Black parents to go to a White neighborhood?" Frank Rennie answered:

> The district started to think about theme schools. This town tends to be seen as an artsy town. We have a lot of artists in it, and we have a lot of well-educated people. Black and White. We have people in the media, in the arts, actors, writers. So they decided to make Hillside School an attraction by putting an arts magnet there. And what does Hillside School have that the other schools don't have? Dance, art, music teachers, youth drum corps. They wanted to attract White parents badly. And White parents were attracted to something like that.

Conversely, Bradford, a traditionally White elementary school in the northern part of town, was to become a magnet for the "basics," aimed at appealing to Black parents who had expressed a desire for their children to concentrate on fundamental skills.

Federal funding was received to aid the development of the magnet schools. The physical structures of elementary schools Nishuane and Bradford were finally improved to the levels of the schools in the northern part of town.

The magnet school plan worked to the point where 2,500 students were voluntarily bused—more than had been bused under the Plan of Action. Racial balance exceeded the 25% figure in all schools, with 28% being the lowest and 54% the highest "minority" presence.

For the 1978–79 school year, the "green" plan was extended to the two middle schools. Glenfield, in the southern part of town, also became a "gifted and talented" magnet school. Mt. Hebron, in the northern part of town, was designated a "fundamental" magnet. Glenfield also received renovations similar to those at Nishuane and Hillside the previous year. To further sweeten the pot for White parents, the creative arts program was moved from Mt. Hebron to Glenfield. Once again it worked and Montclair emerged as a model magnet school system.

The process of creating a system of magnet schools was completed under Superintendent Mary Lee Fitzgerald. Fitzgerald, who replaced Marks in 1981, magnetized all schools, with Edgemont, in 1987, becoming a Montessori School. Fitzgerald remembers her days as Superintendent vividly.

> When I first came, a lot of people didn't want to go to these schools in Montclair. They were worried about integration. Unless you wanted to [go to] Nishuane, which was gifted and talented, a lot of people in town just didn't think it was a good idea. I really do believe after 10 years of working at this, people came to see that you could create real high-quality schools in a town like Montclair. And guess what? They were integrated. People were not moving here in spite of integration. They were not moving out because of integration. They were moving here because of it. That's how we were marketing ourselves.

In 1989, the Educational Testing Service lauded Montclair's magnet school choice program for its success, as determined by "test scores, enrollments and census figures and qualitative data." The researchers concluded:

> Montclair's schools achieved a better racial balance with the magnet plan. In the 1988–89 school year, 48% of the elementary school students were minorities. The range of each school's minority enrollment for the year was between 26%

and 52%. In the previous 10 years, the rate of minority enrollment in different elementary schools ranged between 12% and 74%. The minority representation in individual classrooms was consistent—with one exception. Minority students were underrepresented in advanced classes, especially at the high school and middle school levels. (Educational Testing Service, 1989, p. 1).

A few years later, the Office of Civil Rights of the United States Department of Education voiced similar concerns, particularly with respect to the differential placement of students in rigorous courses and in special education classes by race and gender (Fields, 1996).

Tracking or ability groupings, like special education placements, are deeply connected to race and class. And these politics are often part and parcel of integration plans, in anticipation of "White flight." When combined with differential expectations of students by race and ethnicity, on the part of faculty, these two persistent features of educational inequity have, according to many national scholars and many of our interviewees, worked to maintain racial and class segregation and achievement gaps within presumably desegregated buildings.

Jane Manners told the students in her interview:

Tracking is when you separate students by [what are thought to be] ability levels and you say, "Well, these kids are really, really smart and we're going to put them in this class. And these kids aren't so smart, so we're going to put them in this class." But sometimes a kid who is really smart but maybe he doesn't talk so much, gets put in a [less smart] class; there are not really good measures of how smart that student is and what happens is a lot of times each track tends to break down along racial lines, so I think that there is a lot of racial segregation according to classroom level now.

Renee Baskerville provided a student perspective on the question of tracking.

Oftentimes, either because of poor preparation up until that point or whatever the reasons were, I found that the [upper level/predominantly White] classrooms were "working" on a higher level, were not always as integrated as some of the other classrooms. So they were working toward trying to find

*a good solution for a problem that existed for many years.
But I [sometimes] had a problem because other Black families—Negro families just to keep the language correct—at the
time often ridiculed me and actually made me feel bad for
being a bright student and being a good athlete. And even
other Negro students who were my classmates, they made
fun of me; because they would say things like, "Oh, she
thinks she's White" or "She thinks she's better than other
people." There were many things that were tried and later
became mistakes. As parents began to question, why is it
that in your top classes you have one or two Negro students
and however many White students? Answers. People were
trying to find answers.*

Frank Rennie remarks on differential teacher expectations that
accompanied and undermined integration.

*As principal I might find a teacher—a White teacher—who
was mistreating Black kids and you find out, then you deal
with the teacher. You would also find Black teachers who
dealt very harshly with Black kids....On the part of [all of
these] teachers, I would say because many of them had
stereotypic views in their head....We fired people, some
resigned. You can't ignore the fact that some teachers would
give Black kids poor grades for "discipline."*

Mindy Thompson Fullilove, now a nationally recognized psychiatrist who grew up in segregated elementary schools, not in
Montclair but in Orange, New Jersey, was one of the first
African American children to integrate Hayward School. In her
interview, Fullilove reminded students of the typically unacknowledged pain and loss associated with integration, especially for African American children:

*My father was a union organizer for many years. In the
1950s, there was a senator named Joseph McCarthy who
started a series of Congressional investigations searching for
Communists, and many organizations like unions and civil
rights organizations were destroyed in the process.... My
dad's union fell apart and he lost his job. The FBI would
come and say, "That guy's a troublemaker, don't hire him."
He was depressed because he was unemployed and inactive.
To get him going again, my mom said, "Do you know the*

schools in our town are segregated?" My father said, "Well, we have to fight and get rid of these neighborhood racial lines." So he was the organizer for the school fight in our town. He got the neighbors organized and told this story to the papers and led the struggle to get the schools desegregated.

[At my all-Black school], it was said that the school had bad textbooks and pages torn. But I had really wonderful teachers. I was at the top of my class. I really felt part of the group. All the teachers made it clear they loved us. [Then I was transferred to Hayward for desegregation.] Some of my White teachers [at Hayward] made it clear that they didn't love us...and when you're a little kid in third or fourth grade, you want your teachers to love you.... I just felt all by myself. And I think I didn't know how to fit in. So I was really miserable...and it took me a long time to get over that feeling.

Bernadette Anand, long known and recognized for her brilliant work on educational excellence and equity, in particular her struggle to detrack the English curriculum at the high school, explains the continual struggle against tracking that persists throughout integrated districts nationally.

When I started teaching at the high school, I found a [rigid] tracking system...when I walked into English 9-1A (the highest honors ninth-grade course), which was supposed to be the top-level course, there were only two Black students out of 33 students. When I had to observe in the 10-2 classes and in the bottom-track class, I found all African American students with the exception of maybe two White students. So I said, "We don't leave our prejudices at the school-house door. We walk in with them and we've got to do something about them." But every time we educators would meet and try to change these [tracking procedures], the administration would say, "There will be White flight from the school."

When we finally detracked ninth-grade English at the high school, people would come to the meetings and shout and scream at me...run Camcorders and play the Camcorders at the meetings...they would write letters about me and the course. I was fine when I would teach their upper-track stu-

dents, but then later I became the worst possible educator who couldn't possibly teach to a class of all different kinds of kids. So they thought I would dumb-down the curriculum. They were very upset because we believed in a multicultural curriculum [see Fields, 1996; Fine, Anand, Jordan, & Sherman, 2000; Karp, 1993; for a history, see Off Track *video, Fine, Anand, Hancock, Jordan, & Sherman, 1998].*

The struggles to authentically integrate schools, classrooms, and curricula—not merely desegregate, as Michael Johnson has noted, and Mindy Fullilove, Bernadette Anand, Frank Rennie, Judy Miller, and so many others have testified—are ongoing. And today districts like Montclair confront budget cuts from the federal and state governments, which drastically undermine efforts for quality education and desegregation. The most recent cuts in aid to Montclair remind us of the words of activist Walter Lack.

> To the extent that we succeed in educating our children, we provide the life blood for our country's future. To the extent we fail, we create a burden in the form of people unable to provide for themselves.... Benjamin Franklin once said, "The only thing more expensive than education is ignorance." (*Montclair Times*, May 17, 1984)

It was a long and mostly forgotten struggle for desegregation that was fought in Montclair. It is a struggle that most of us would not know about had it not been for the Renaissance students. But 24 years after *Brown* v. *Board of Education* and 21 years after federal troops forced the integration of Little Rock, Arkansas, schools, Montclair also integrated its school buildings. Renaissance students during the 1998–99 school year interviewed the real heroes of this story, documenting the struggles, lessons, and victories. Among the words, wisdom, contradictions, and legacies of ambivalence they collected the following:

School desegregation had a very positive effect on this town. No one can ignore it anymore, sweep it under the rug, kind of go along living their very segregated existence, not thinking about the other race. It forced the town to be Black and White, like much more equal opportunity than before. (Mary Lee Fitzgerald)

It couldn't have been easy for kids that age to hear the things I was saying about their town, which is always being described as the greatest place where everyone mixes and mingles. (Lydia Davis Barrett, after her interview with the seventh graders, in Mays, 1998, p. 52)

It should be kept in mind that desegregation and integration are not the same thing. (Michael Johnson)

TABLE 3. Enrollment and Racial Distribution by School and Level 2000–01

	White		Black		Hispanic		Amer. Indian		Asian/Pacific Is.		Total
Elementary Schools	#	%	#	%	#	%	#	%	#	%	
Bradford	197	54.4%	142	39.2%	14	3.9%		0.0%	9	2.5%	362
Edgemont	158	51.8%	101	33.1%	16	5.2%		0.0%	30	9.8%	305
Hillside	267	41.1%	346	53.2%	19	2.9%	4	0.6%	14	2.2%	650
Nishuane	294	47.0%	302	48.3%	20	3.2%		0.0%	9	1.4%	625
Northeast	145	40.6%	158	44.3%	37	10.4%		0.0%	17	4.8%	357
DLC	16	50.0%	14	43.8%	0	0.0%		0.0%	2	6.3%	32
Rand	196	54.0%	130	35.8%	24	6.6%	3	0.8%	10	2.8%	363
Watchung	244	55.3%	151	34.2%	21	4.8%	2	0.5%	23	5.2%	441
Total	1,517	48.4%	1,344	42.9%	151	4.8%	9	0.3%	114	3.6%	3,135
Middle Schools											
Glenfield	347	49.3%	313	44.5%	22	3.1%	3	0.4%	19	2.7%	704
Mt. Hebron	191	38.2%	238	47.6%	45	9.0%		0.0%	26	5.2%	500
Renaissance	114	50.7%	91	40.4%	10	4.4%		0.0%	10	4.4%	225
Total	652	45.6%	642	44.9%	77	5.4%	3	0.2%	55	3.8%	1,429
High School	627	40.5%	783	50.6%	70	4.5%		0.0%	67	4.3%	1,547
Grand Total	2,796	45.8%	2,769	45.3%	298	4.9%	12	0.2%	236	3.9%	6,111

Note: Does not include one reported charter school student in Mt. Hebron eighth grade.

And Today...

The history that the seventh graders at the Renaissance Middle School have taught us is significant. It is a story of conflict, persistence, legal battles, and ultimately a community coming together to desegregate its schools through the establishment of a continuing, evolving magnet system. The creation of the Renaissance School is itself only the latest development in a system that must remain determined and flexible in developing compelling themes where equity and excellence sit side-by-side.

A generation after the fight to desegregate, Montclair's public schools reflect the racial composition of the student population at each specific level. Despite recent significant losses in state aid and soaring property taxes, there is little talk of ending the expensive busing program that allows the magnet system to exist. Most significant, the coded cries for neighborhood schools that would destroy this racial balance have not been heard for a long time. Table 3 illustrates the current distribution of students, by race and ethnicity, across schools and grade levels.

While the story presented by the Renaissance students could end here, doing so would be a disservice to these students, to the community, and to the ongoing racial struggles across America. No one can, or should, deny that the hard fought victories were impressive. Today there are no separate public schools for White students in the southwestern and northern parts of town nor are there inherently unequal "Negro" schools housed in Nishuane and Glenfield. Montclair must be proud of these changes and proud of its own students for uncovering the story. As Helen Newhouse told the students:

> *I think immense progress has been made. The magnet school system seems to operate very successfully...what I hear from young parents is all favorable. And Black and White children certainly do go to school together peacefully and happily and socialize together. We have a working model of integrated schools, even though there is still some residential segregation.*

However, the struggle for racial justice, in housing and in schools, will never be over. A closer look at Table 3 reflects a disturbing trend. The percentage of White students drops at each level. For elementary schools the proportion of White students is 48.4%. This figure drops to 45.6% for middle schools and 40.5% for the high school. Put bluntly, the middle schools and the high school are progressively losing a proportion of White students. Indeed, many charge that throughout the system, but within the high school most particularly, it is the tracking system, or what some prefer to call a system of "ability grouping," that produces another form of segregation. The Montclair public schools are maintaining racial balance within the system and within the schools, but often not in the particular classrooms at the high or low end of academic rigor. As Judy Miller told the students:

> I think that Montclair has, you know, a ways to go. It has made a great deal of progress and is very proud of itself. There is a lot of activity...a lot of culture. People in recent years have moved to Montclair because they wanted the kind of open experience for their children, which is good... the possibility of good experience, a good social experience. But we have a very long ways to go. The struggle is ongoing.

The story told by the Renaissance students is a true story, but it is also a chapter in a longer epic that is still unfolding. Montclair, as it did with the desegregation battle of a generation ago, must continue to struggle with issues of White flight, middle-class flight, tracking, and racial justice in its schools. With a rich history of activism, Montclair is well positioned to take up these issues, which most of America has left behind. Actor Frankie Faison articulates the pride, the ambivalence, and the challenge that constitute Montclair.

> The best thing we've done here is to put people in a community together. Is it working perfectly? Of course not. But we're trying to deal with the issues. And for that alone, I can't think of any place I'd rather be.

Montclair Wrong for Too Long: The Youth Researchers Speak

Once we completed the interviews, and the transcriptions, coding, and write-ups, the Renaissance students decided that they, indeed, should interview each other and have the final say. They were determined to title this section "Montclair Wrong for Too Long," to reveal their distress at "what has been," and their sense of possibility for "what must be."

As the future of America, they wanted us to know:

[The] project taught me that Montclair wasn't always the beautiful town it is now. Twenty to thirty years ago, it still looked beautiful but with demons on the inside which grow smaller with every effort to integrate.
Sankho

There are still schools in Montclair that tend to have a bit more Black people in them, and there are still schools that tend to have a bit more White people. I believe Montclair has made wonderful progress toward integration. If it weren't for integration, I'd be a totally different person.   Jeremy

[I learned] that people went through a lot to integrate the schools and desegregate the town. And the fact that it wasn't just Black people who wanted to desegregate, it was also the Whites.   Jordan

I think it has been good but some schools have a majority of White or Black children still. Like in Littleton, Colorado, only one student was Black and he was one of the kids they tracked down.
Jordan

I learned that people would give their lives and all their time just to see laws be fair on all races, and to see a friendship or no hesitations to another race, basically because they just wanted to be in a normal world.
Gabe

Since 1970, we have made (almost) great progress in becoming integrated. It took courage.
Charmecia

There is much more to the history of this town. [I used] to think that it was so far away. The struggle is still alive; Montclair has a very deep history of desegregation and has struggled and has had a very strong impact on our nation's struggle for equality.   Alex B.

[I learned] that at one point in time there was social hatred.   Eric

I learned that Montclair wasn't integrated one bit back in the day. I thought Montclair schools were always integrated. I'm growing up going to schools that are integrated, I never knew about the struggle…

Matt K.

It's good, in every school I have been to here I have seen a mixture of all different kinds of cultures. In my class alone there are Caucasians, African Americans, Indians, and many mixtures of other cultures. I could not even start to imagine what it would be like to live in an all-White community.

Samantha

I think people should be aware of all cultures, not just African American. Sometimes people are racist against Caucasians, Indians, and White people.

Chloe K.

Yes, storeowners are stereotyping people, especially African Americans. There is not much of a mix of other cultures either. Indians, Latinos, and other people are looked at differently than everyone else. Ageism and sexism are also very prominent in Montclair. One day when I, Stephanie, and Landon get to visit our old teachers, we stopped at a store to buy gum. Stephanie and I, who are White, walked around the store freely, but Landon, on the other hand, was followed closely. He is an African American male.

Liesje

They made good progress. There is now integration in the schools. Some Montclair people said that there should be integration in the schools, while others said that the schools should stay the way they are. The people that wanted integration fought all the way through and they won. So I'm happy for what these people did for us.

Channing

I think that the areas that need to be worked on are not only among racial lines, but include the special education students…. When I was in the first grade, there was a special education student who came to picture day all dressed up in a suit ready for the class picture and the teacher walked up to him and said you can't take the picture with this class, you have to do it with the special education class.

Dana J.

The stores are still racist. For example, some people don't trust African Americans because of their color and how they dress.   Stephanie

Now we need to integrate our town and our neighborhoods.   Henry

If we don't act now then the town will slowly disintegrate, until we have nothing left and all the effort people put in and died for will go to waste.
                              Alex B.

The project taught me that if you want something done, *you can't give up.* You have to work hard for it.
                              Andretta

KEEPING THE STRUGGLE ALIVE

A Teacher's Guide to the Oral History Project

How the Project Began

At Renaissance Middle School, the latest district magnet, we boast of an integrated curriculum delivered through themes that are connected to the community of Montclair. Courses are created with this end in mind. As a faculty, we make every effort to build on the rich diversity, history, and experience the town has to offer. The theme "Movements and Migrations" was a natural fit for the story of Montclair's struggle for school integration. Since seventh graders had explored several historical movements, including the Civil Rights Movement, the Labor Movement, the Women's Movement, and the Westward Movement, we decided that we would offer a 9-week oral history course for each of four seventh-grade sections. This course would be given on Fridays when we have extended teaching periods of 2¼ hours. It would result in a publication containing the oral histories we would gather over the course of the year.

As educators, we asked the needed structural questions and formed a course outline.

What is the goal of the course?

Students will conduct 30 interviews of people involved in Montclair's school desegregation efforts and document and present these oral histories in book form to be shared with the school and local community.

What resources will we use and why?

Articles from the *Montclair Times*, documents from the Montclair Board of Education, films and books that provide a national historical perspective, and the stories of the many Montclair residents associated with the town's desegregation efforts would provide the background information needed for the project.

What do we want the students to be able to do as a result of this course?

We want the students to be able to conduct an interview, write an accurate account of the interview, engage in active listening on discussions of race, understand and apply the essential elements of other movements to the one under study, and reflect on the current educational system in light of the many plans to integrate the Montclair public schools through a magnet program.

We knew the power of ice cream, Dunkin' Donuts, hot chocolate, and assorted goodies to motivate 12- and 13-year-olds, but we wanted to be sure our curriculum offered our diversified learners a place where they would feel safe while exploring issues of race and power in their own lives and those of community members. We approached our students with imagination, because, as Maxine Greene reminds us,

> Imagination allows us to cross the empty spaces between ourselves and those we teachers have called 'other' over the years. If those others are willing to give us clues, we can look in some manner through strangers' eyes and hear through their ears and give credence to alternative realities (Greene, 1995, p. 3).

THE CLASS MEETINGS

Beginning Session

One way to begin examining oral histories is to have middle school students reflect on the differences between oral and written history.

- We asked the class to respond in writing to the following sentence stub: Oral history is...; it is not...
- Each student shared his/her responses, which were recorded on two pieces of newsprint.

was from 1947, Brandon exclaimed, "Dag, that's old. My father wasn't even born then." We reminded Brandon that he might be entering dangerous territory; one of us was familiar with the time.

We then had students examine the *Montclair Times* articles more closely to

- Read emotionally and racially charged words to understand how these words are connected to stereotyping, prejudice, and privilege.
- See where articles and headlines were placed and what the implications might be.
- Talk about the photos used and determine what they represented.

Weeks Two and Three

We were interested in having our students connect the local events in Montclair to the national Civil Rights Movement and the struggle for school integration. During these next two meetings, we gave students an accurate historical context for their oral history project by having them read Jim Haskins's sensitive, student-friendly book *Separate But Not Equal: The Dream and the Struggle*. We read aloud Chapter 12, "The Supreme Court Decides," to hear about the famous *Brown* v. *Board of Education* case and how it was argued. We attended to specific quotes from the chapter and asked the students to discuss what the actual words meant and why they were essential to the understanding of the Supreme Court decision.

> To separate [Black children] from others of similar age and qualifications solely because of their race generates a feeling of inferiority as to their status in the community that may affect their hearts and minds in a way unlikely ever to be undone.
>
> We conclude that in the field of public education the doctrine of separate but equal has no place. Separate educational facilities are inherently unequal. (Haskins, 1998, p. 137)

We built on the new knowledge by reading "Little Rock, Arkansas," another chapter from Jim Haskins's book. Before our actual class reading, we asked the students to talk about how they arrived at school each day: who is on the street when they arrive, how these people feel about them, as students how do they enter the school, how do they feel in the halls, in the class-rooms, cafeteria, and bathrooms, and how are they treated by their classmates and teachers. After the discussion, the students read about the nine students who integrated Central High School in Little Rock, Arkansas. We contrasted the experiences by having the students

- Write a journal entry such as one that might have been entered by one of the Black students at Little Rock on the night of September 3, 1957, the day the nine integrated the school.
- Share these journal entries and talk about their feelings, questions, and comments.

PBS's fourth episode of *Eyes on the Prize* (1986) provided a further deepening of the historical context. The live footage shot the day the nine Black students integrated Little Rock offered a powerful view of racism and those who espouse it.

- Students reflected on Thurgood Marshall's words, "There is some magic in it. You can have them voting together, you can have them not restricted because of law in the houses they live in. You can have them going to the same state university and the same college, but if they go to elementary and high school together, the world will fall apart." They asked, Why?
- We discussed the cycle of oppression and how it continues to keep itself in motion.
- We grappled with how the cycle can be broken. We asked who and what interrupts the cycle and how we are sure we are hearing their voices.

We decided to call on the rich history of one of our town residents, Arthur Kinoy, Professor Emeritus at Rutgers School of Law and one of the great civil rights lawyers of our time. Our students were captivated by Mr. Kinoy's stories of how he met Ella Baker and Dr. King as he defended their civil rights.

Jane Manners, a former Montclair High School graduate, wrote her senior thesis at Harvard College on the history of the Montclair magnet school system. After reading her article in *Race Traitor*, we contacted Jane and she agreed to an interview. Students tapped into Jane's research; their knowledge base was expanding.

We proceeded to read the actual suit Montclair parents brought against the Board of Education on behalf of their children. The students took notice of a specific family name, Baskerville.

- Students asked if Charles and Marjorie Baskerville were related to Ali, their classmate. To their surprise, Ali tells the class the Baskervilles are his grandparents. Ali's mother, Dr. Renee Baskerville, is one of the children on whose behalf the suit was brought before the Board of Education.

We noted that primary documents offer students the opportunity to think critically and to recognize the filtering effects of secondary sources. A lot of questions got asked. What was happening? What were the schools like?

We offered charts, profiles, and graphs detailing the racial profiles of the schools and the community. We asked the students to analyze the racial makeup of the schools in relation to total enrollment. We showed them the current racial profiles of both the schools and the community housing patterns and asked if anything had changed.

Week Four

We returned to the *Montclair Times* articles, scanning them for people connected to our community's integration efforts. The students were eager to contact them and arrange for interview times and places.

Some of the students argued that there might be others who were involved in the struggle who were not mentioned in the newspaper. These students decided to write an article for the *Montclair Times* explaining their project and requesting that those who had information please contact the school.

Here was another opportunity to teach specific writing skills; this time newspaper writing was the focus. Instruction in interviewing techniques continued during this week's session. We talked about how to meet people, introduce oneself, hold the microphone, ask questions, and cultivate the art of encouraging those who are being interviewed to expand on a topic, share a story, or shorten answers. Students practiced by interviewing each other about a variety of topics and in a variety of circumstances.

We proceeded to help students formulate the questions we would ask of our guests, who would visit the classroom over the next few Fridays. We made certain to involve all students in the interviewing and helped them with the actual process. We had them reflect at the end of each session after they had the chance to hear three or four individuals. As collaborators, we talked during break time about the perspectives, differences, and similarities of the people we interviewed. More questions were presented to the students. We decided as a class how to move the research forward in our next session.

James Meredith, flanked by federal officials, begins his college career at the University of Mississippi in 1962. The university was previously segregated but ordered by a federal court to accept Meredith, instigating days of violence and rioting by whites.

Weeks Five, Six, and Seven

We arranged for four or five interviews for each of the sessions. Prior to our meetings, we reviewed our questions, talked about the background of each of our guests, and decided whether we would keep some of the questions we developed, add some more, or delete a few. Students volunteered to ask our guests the questions they wanted addressed. We alternated questioners during each of the interviews to involve all students.

After each set of interviews, we stopped and asked students to reflect on each of the interviews. Were the stories similar? Were the interviewees' experiences similar or different? Why or why not? What roles did the adults play in the history of Montclair's desegregation efforts? Were there personal costs each had to pay?

After all of the possible interviews were held and transcribed, we engaged the students in a discussion of how we should organize the book. They decided on the title *Montclair Wrong for Too Long: A History of Montclair's Desegregation* and established three main chapter headings to help them organize the interview material: Housing, Social Life, and The Schools. All of the people they had interviewed addressed one or more of these areas.

We placed a call for help to Sheila Crowell and Ellen Kolba, directors of the Writers' Room, a nationally acclaimed program that trains volunteers to serve as writing coaches in our district's schools. Sheila and Ellen offered suggestions about how the students could take what they had transcribed and select carefully and accurately the sections they wanted to include in the book. Writing coaches worked with the students to help them revise and refine their work.

Tiffany Perkins, a doctoral candidate at CUNY, organized the oral history material into themes, including community life before integration, school before integration, protests and the struggle for integration, resistance and victories, and schools since integration. Dr. David S. Surrey, anthropologist and faculty member at St. Peter's College, researched and created the historical background into which the Montclair story has been placed.

At the end of the project, we had the students interview each other to find out whether they thought that real progress had been made toward Montclair's goals of integration. We wanted to know if there were areas where work still needed to be done and what challenges lay ahead. The last question asked for a personal assessment of the project and the lessons it taught. As Jeremy stated, "I never knew how segregated Montclair used to be and just how current that 'used to be' was."

Acknowledgments

WE WOULD LIKE TO THANK THOSE who made this work possible. First and foremost we express our gratitude to all of the guests who gave freely of their time as they told their personal stories and memories: Marlene Anderson, Lydia Davis Barrett, Marjorie Baskerville, Renee Baskerville, Mary Lee Fitzgerald, Joseph Fortunato, Mindy Thompson Fullilove, Michael Johnson, Walter Lack, Jane Manners, Judith Miller, Helen Newhouse, Frank Rennie, Joan Smith, and Nancy Winkler.

We are also grateful to Rajive Anand, who pored through the record of Montclair's written history for cogent articles and news stories; Kim Craft, Marsha Kalman, Rachel Serlen, and Ellen Kolba for hours of coaching students as they worked with interview transcripts; Ronald Ridgeway, Gloria Cheng, Ann Marie Scarpa, and Shea Little of Ronald Ridgeway Inc., for help with format and graphics; Renaissance teacher Bette Baronco-Bland for her constant encouragement and support; Lise Funderburg, who spent hours with us as we worked and then took our story to the world through the *New York Times*; the Spencer Foundation and Carnegie Foundation for much needed monetary support; school secretary Mary Ann Reid; and, lastly, the extended Renaissance family that believes in integrated education.

KEEPING THE STRUGGLE ALIVE

Student Contributors

Adelman, Eric
Adelson, Erna
Alves, Nefertiti
Ball, Alex
Bandes, Ian
Baskerville, Ali
Bouknight, Candace
Brown, Channing
Carter-Robinson, Ashley
Christovao, Jane
Cochran, Peter
Cohen-Serrins, Lissadel
Delaney, Jordan
Dennis, Chandler
DeSalvo, Jeremy
Glover, Landon
Gonzalez, Charmecia
Granger, Norman
Gutelle, Chloe
Halper, Zack
Harris, Olivia
Hodgson, Liesje
Huling, Travis
Jones, Dana
Kastner, Anna
Katz, Chloe
Kelly-Sordolet, Kaelan
Kennedy, Matt
Kerr, Michael
Kuhl, Nick
Landis, Alex
Lands, Kelly
Lee, Andrea
Mallik, Sankho

Marrs, Diana
Mauro, Katie
McKoy, Travis
Miscia, Dana
Moss, Alison
Mullarney, Chelsea
Mumby, Ryan
Narcise, Kenny
O'Brien, Nick
Peroff, Alex
Polo, Susanna
Richardson, Evan
Richardson, Michelle
Rezvani, Robert
Richman, Samantha
Robins, Stephanie
Sage-El, Trevor
Sargent, Emanuel
Seltzer, Henry
Shelton, Daryl
Smith, Brandon
Stephens, Danny
Stewart, Jack
Stone-Jansen, Gabe
Taylor, Andretta
Thomas, Robert
Tribble, Matt
Unger, Becca
Urdang, Kendra
Walia, Qurban
White, Bryan
White, Caroline
White, Kenneth
Wyatt, Chase

KEEPING THE STRUGGLE ALIVE

References

Adams, J. [Superintendent]. (1972). *A plan of action.* Montclair Board of Education.

Aronowitz, S., & Giroux, H. A. (1993). *Education still under siege* (2nd ed.). South Hadley, MA: Bergin & Garvey.

Baldwin, J. (1961). Fifth Avenue, Uptown: A letter from Harlem. In *Nobody knows my name: More notes of a Native Son.* New York: Dial Press.

Bell, D. (1987). *And we are not saved: The elusive quest for racial justice.* New York: Basic Books.

Dewey, J. (1938). *Experience and education.* New York: Touchstone.

Educational Testing Service. (1999, August 14). *Montclair Magnet School Choice Program Successful.*

Eyes on the Prize [PBS Video], Episode 4. (1986). Boston: Blackside.

Fields, W. (1996, November/December). The myth of Montclair. *New Jersey Reporter, 26*(4), 16–21.

Fine, M., Anand, B., Hancock, M., Jordan, C., & Sherman, D. (1998). *Off track* [video]. New York: Teachers College Press.

Fine, M., Anand, B., Jordan, C., & Sherman, D. (2000). Before the bleach gets us all. In L. Weis, & M. Fine (Eds.), *Construction sites* (pp. 161–179). New York: Teachers College Press.

Foster, M. (1997). *Black teachers on teaching.* New York: New Press.

Freire, P. (1998). *Teachers as cultural workers: Letters to those who dare teach.* Boulder, CO: Westview Press.

Greene, M. (2001). *Variations on a blue guitar: The Lincoln Center Institute lectures on aesthetic education.* New York: Teachers College Press.

Greene, M. (1995). *Releasing the imagination: Essays on education, the arts and social change.* San Francisco: Jossey-Bass.

Greene, M. (1993). Diversity and inclusion. *Teachers College Record, 2,* 211–221.

Greene, M. (1988). *The dialectic of freedom.* New York: Teachers College Press.

Haskins, J. (1998). *Separate but not equal: The dream and the struggle.* New York: Scholastic.

Horowitz, C. (1996, November 18). The upper west side of suburbia. *New York Magazine,* pp. 43–49.

Karp, S. (1993). Many pieces to the detracking puzzle. *Rethinking Schools, 8,* 16–17.

Ladson-Billings, G. (1998). Who will survive America? In D. Carlson & M. W. Apple (Eds.), *Power/knowledge/pedagogy: The meaning of democratic education in unsettling times* (pp. 289–304). Boulder, CO: Westview Press.

Levine, E. (1993). *Freedom's children: Young civil rights activists tell their own stories.* New York: Avon.

Manners, J. (1998). Repackaging segregation: The history of the magnet school system in Montclair, NJ. *Race Traitor, 8*, 51–97.

Mays, J. (1998, December). Once upon a time in the Montclair Schools. *Sunday Star Ledger*, pp. 49, 52.

McLemore, S., Dale, H. R., & Baker, S. G. (2000). *Race and ethnic relations in America* (6th ed.). Boston: Allyn & Bacon.

Meier, D. (1995). *The power of their ideas: Lessons for America from a small school in Harlem.* Boston: Beacon Press.

Milliken, E. (n.d.). The early history of Saint Peter Claver Church, 1931–1939. South Orange, NJ: Seton Hall University.

Mooney, J. (2001, July 18). N.J. school segregation grows worse. *The Star Ledger.*

New Jersey Department of Education. (1996, May). *Core curriculum content standards.*

Oakes, J. (1985). *Keeping track: How schools structure inequality.* New Haven: Yale University Press.

Orfield, G., Easton, S., & the Harvard Project on School Desegregation. (1996). *Dismantling desegregation: The quiet reversal of* Brown *v.* Board of Education. New York: New Press.

Orfield, G., & Yun, J. (1999). *Resegregation in American schools* (The Civil Rights Project). Cambridge, MA: Harvard University Press.

powell, j. (1999, December). Educational Integration Initiatives Project, University of Minnesota and Joyce Foundation.

Shaw, T. (1996, February 7). Brown was bigger than test scores. *Education Week*, p. 42.

Taylor, M. (1976). *Roll of thunder, hear my cry.* New York: Puffin.

Wheelock, A. (1992). *Crossing the tracks.* New York: New Press.

Index

About the Authors

Bernadette Anand serves on the faculty of Bank Street Graduate School of Education. An educator for over 40 years, she has taught at all grade levels and served as a middle school principal. She founded Renaissance School, Montclair, New Jersey's newest public magnet where she served as both principal and teacher.

A strong proponent of collaborative and experiential learning, Dr. Anand promotes diversity of voices both in the classroom and in the curriculum. Her most recent collaboration with Michelle Fine, Carlton Jordan, and Dana Sherman is the documentary film, *Off-Track* (Teachers College Press, 1998), exploring an innovative multicultural English program for ninth grade students at Montclair High School.

She has led both professional and community workshops and seminars on building common ground. A graduate of Caldwell College, Bernadette Anand earned her M.A. from Providence College and her doctorate from New York University.

Michelle Fine is a professor of social psychology at CUNY, The Graduate Center. Her recent books include *The Unknown City* (with Lois Weis), *Off-White* (with Lois Weis, Linda Powell, and Mun Wong), *Becoming Gentlemen* (with Lani Guinier), and *Construction Sites* and *Speed Bumps* (both with Lois Weis, Teachers College Press). She also helped to create the 30-minute, teacher- and adolescent-friendly video *Off-Track* (Teachers College Press, 1998).

David S. Surrey is a professor of urban studies and sociology at St. Peter's College. For ten years he was also the College's director of the Institute for the Advancement of Urban Education in which pre-K through college institutions collaborated on interdisciplinary curriculum development. He is the author of *Choice of Conscience: Vietnam Era Draft and Military Resisters in Canada,* and several articles on youth culture in urban America.

Tiffany Perkins, M.A., is currently a Ph.D. candidate in the Social-Personality Psychology program at the City University of New York Graduate School. This book further contributes to her research interests around adolescents and social injustices, where the hope is to give a voice to children who typically do not have a voice, such as children of mothers with mental retardation. Ms. Perkins has contributed to numerous chapters, articles, presentations, and technical reports related to adolescents and social injustices, specifically around issues of disability, including a report submitted to NSF on providing hands-on science activities to blind and hearing-impaired children titled *Evaluation of "playtime is science" for children who are blind and visually impaired: You don't need to be sighted to be a scientist, do you?;* an IASSID (International Association for the Scientific Study of Intellectual Disability) presentation titled "Children whose mothers have mental retardation: What happens when the child has no cognitive impairment?"; and a revision of Education Equity Concept's *Building Community II: A Manual Exploring Issues of Women and Disability,* exploring the treatment of girls and women with disabilities in educational, occupational, and healthcare settings.